Thierry Geerts

DIGI

How to reinvent

TA

the world

LIS

LANNOO

Contents

© iStock

Europe, the capital of Digitalis?
With CERN, the European Organization for Nuclear Research,
Europe is already a front-runner when it comes to scientific research.

Introduction

Welcome to Digitalis

September 2016. If we were to believe the press, a countless number of jobs are threatened by the digital evolution. A shock wave rattled Belgium when Caterpillar announced the shutdown of its local factory, leaving 2200 workers without a job. All throughout Europe we are aware of long series of bad news related to restructuring operations and layoffs. Every employee termination plan makes the front page of the newspapers for days on end. "Digitalization threatens employment," is what we are repeatedly told. Yet, in most European countries, more people than ever before in history have a job to go to. This means that the number of jobs being created is greater than the number of jobs being lost. The employment market is doing a lot better than we are made to believe due to the number of planned layoffs. But, positive information gets lost in the flow of bad news. And this contributes heavily to the fact that 500 million Europeans are worried about their futures and blaming digitalization.

Personally, I've felt totally at ease in the digital world for over twenty years now. For the last six years I've been directing the Belgium and Luxembourg operations of Google, one of the most innovative companies operating in the digital arena. Before joining this company, I worked for fifteen years for the Belgian media group Corelio (now Mediahuis), which publishes daily newspapers such as *De Standaard* and *Het Nieuwsblad*. Digital projects rapidly became the core of my missions. These different experiences have allowed me to become a privileged observer of the upheavals in the world around us. The subject matter of this book doesn't concern Google, but represents my personal view based on my experience and deeply held beliefs. I strongly believe that digitalization offers opportunities to Europe and its citizens and that it is very important to seize these opportunities now.

As digitalization intensifies, unfortunately I feel that many people are overcome by anxiety, causing populism, nationalism and protectionism to resurface. This could be explained by the huge lack of understanding of the society in which we live and of the way it has changed profoundly over a very short time. It's all linked to the speed of digitalization, but we shouldn't fear it. Don't get me wrong: risks do exist. The digital revolution can make us immortal, but it can also have disastrous consequences if we don't deal with it properly. It's the characteristic of every great technological evolution.

Welcome to Digitalis, a land in which 4 billion people are connected thanks to the internet.

Nuclear technology made it possible to revolutionize medicine but it also created the atomic bomb. If we want to fully seize the chances that digital technologies are offering us, it really is necessary to get the right information about what's happening in the world to as many people as possible. That's why I invite you to follow me to Digitalis, a land in which 4 billion of people are connected thanks to the internet. Digitalis, like every other country, has to face social issues such as health, mobility, education, the economy and many others. The question now is whether we want it to be a wonderful country or one dominated by obscurity, pessimism and stagnation. The choice is ours. Personally, I prefer the first solution and I'm going to take citizens, entrepreneurs and decision makers on a trip through Digitalis to show them everything that's possible. And what stops Europe from becoming the capital of Digitalis? Europe has always been at the forefront of previous industrial revolutions and there is no reason at all for it to stop while things are going so well. The aim of this book is to propose an optimistic alternative solution. Without being naïve, but in a constructive way: technological progress offers a unique opportunity to approach society's fundamental issues. There are no miracle solutions; it's up to us, both women and men, to make the right choices. I call it "possibilism": understanding what's possible increases the chances of making it happen. We shouldn't be guided by fear but rather by the conviction that it is possible to build a better world. Sundar Pichai, Google's CEO, said it best: "I'm optimistic about technology, not because I believe in technology, but because I believe in people and humanity."

"I'm optimistic about technology. Not because I believe in technology, but because I believe in people and humanity."

Part 1 _____ The world we live in

CHAPTER 1

An era of abundance and knowledge

Every era has been marked by technological innovation. This current period points to unusual issues that are at stake. With this digital revolution we are in the midst of a new industrial revolution. Fears are also fueled because each new technology encounters resistance. The very first trains couldn't go any faster than 100 km/hour. People thought that crossing this symbolic limit could be mortal. In the beginning, a person had to walk in front of the train waving a red flag. Today, we are constantly bombarded by these kinds of innovations. To illustrate the pace of evolution, the French philosopher Michel Serre refers to the dictionary of the *Academie Française*. In the past, an average of three to four thousand words were added or deleted from each edition (every 20 to 25 years). In the most recent edition this has increased to 37,000 words. The same is true for other languages, e.g. for Swedish.[1] Never in history has language experienced such evolution; and language reflects our society. It's precisely because we are subject to so many new developments that it's important to understand what's happening and how to approach it. It's the only way to make sure Digitalis is peaceful country where one can live well.

The future is brighter than we think

If I were to mention a book that has changed my life, it would be: *Abundance: The Future Is Better Than You Think*. *The Economist* qualified this worldwide bestseller as a "a godsend for those who suffer from Armageddon fatigue." I read it in a single sitting during a flight to the United States in 2012. The authors, American journalist Steven Kotler and entrepreneur Peter Diamandis, predict a near-term future marked by abundance. That was all that was needed to generate my interest, as I've grown up in a world that was dominated by the fear of not having enough. I have very clear memories of the oil crisis in the seventies, when people and government leaders alike were obsessed with fuel shortages and its effect on oil prices. In school, our teachers taught us about the horrifying conclusions of the Club of Rome, especially about when the oil supply ran out. By extension, the entire industrial era economy revolves around raw materials: prices are driven up because of their limited availability and how they're used should be thought through thoroughly. The shortage causes limitations and an unequal distribution of wealth. Oil countries are rich and all the others are dependent on them.

> *Humanity is now entering a period of radical transformation in which technology has the potential to significantly raise the basic standards of living for every woman, man, and child on this planet.*

When reading *Abundance*, many pieces of the puzzle started to fall into place. Every fiber of my being knew instinctively that technology could make the world a better place, but I didn't yet grasp to what extent.

In *Abundance* we read: "For the first time in history, our capabilities have begun to catch up to our ambitions. Humanity is now entering a period of radical transformation in which technology has the potential to significantly raise the basic standards of living for every woman, man, and child on this planet. Within a generation we will be able to provide goods and services, once reserved for the wealthy few, to any and all who need them. Or desire them."

Steven Kotler and Peter Diamandis don't pretend that the world will be a place where all of us will be swimming in money or luxury. They describe an endless scope of unfolding possibilities to resolve all of the world's major problems. Let's take energy as an example. All over the world, the task is to move away from oil as the primary energy source. The supply of this resource is running out, it's unequally distributed and it pollutes. The big challenge consists in replacing oil with, for example, solar energy. Skeptics claimed that solar energy would not suffice to make the world and the industry turn. But things have changed. The sun is able to provide, in a single day, more than enough energy to meet our needs for a year. It's abundantly present, its distribution is a lot more equal and the sun doesn't pollute. Not having enough solar energy isn't the problem. No, the challenge is to capture and store all this energy. As soon as we've overcome this difficulty, we'll have access to an endless supply of energy and the energy shortage problem will be a thing of the past. If ten years ago this seemed inconceivable, meanwhile the significance of improved technology is such that that dream is on the verge of becoming a reality. Also, Google's global activities have been completely CO_2 neutral since 2007. And since 2017, the internet company has been operating using 100% renewable energy. Given the fact that data centers are huge consumers of electricity this is a major milestone. All of this is to say that the energy problem is not impossible to solve. Of course, solar energy is not the answer to everything. Thanks to technological progress, wind, hydraulic and geothermal energies can also help us. All of this cannot happen by itself: huge investments are required as well as innovation and infrastructure projects. But when all is said and done, we'll live in a world where there is an abundance of energy.

Solving the energy shortage issue is a first step in the direction of solving other global problems, like the scarcity of clean water. In reality, there's no lack of water on the planet, because approximately 70% of our earth's surface is water. However, 97% of that is salt water and therefore unsuitable for consumption. Technologically it's possible to desalinate seawater, but a tremendous amount of energy would be needed to do so. Not too long ago, it was financially inconceivable, but in the near future when there will be an abundance of energy, it will also be possible to solve the issue of the clean water shortage. An adequate water and energy supply will allow food production for the entire world population and therefore put a hiatus on starvation. Ironically, this will also allow us to deal with the issue of overcrowding. Max Roser, economist at the University of Oxford wrote: "What we have seen in country after country over the last 200 years is that once women realise that the chances of their children dying has declined substantially, they adapt and choose to have fewer children. Population growth then comes to an end." This transition from a high mortality and birth rate to a low mortality and birth rate is known as demographic transition. This is how the number of children per family has undergone a major decrease worldwide over the last 50 years: from an average of five children per family in the early 1960s to the current average of just 2.5. Eventually, the day will come when the world's population will diminish or at least stabilize.

The knowledge economy

The book *Abundance* describes the technological and scientific context of movements operating throughout the world, but it doesn't explain what is happening economically. Despite all of the technological progress, many people feel that they were better off ten years ago. Economic growth is still limited and many businesses seem to be negatively affected by digitalization instead of being able to reap the benefits. It took a YouTube video by the French Idriss Aberkane, sent to me by Annick Vandersmissen, CEO of web agency blue2purple, to understand the importance of digital evolution for our economic model. Idriss Aberkane is a real jack-of-all-trades who manages to analyze the big evolutions in our society. In 2015 he wrote a work titled "Economy of Knowledge", in which he explains how we're moving forward into an economy of knowledge.

Unlike traditional raw materials, we can't run out of knowledge. It's an inexhaustible resource that will never dry up.

"Imagine an economy whose main resource is infinite. Imagine an economy endowed with an intrinsic form of justice, an economy that facilitates and rewards sharing, an economy where the unemployed boast greater purchasing power than those in work, an economy where 1 and 1 makes 3, an economy in which everyone is born with purchasing power and where, ultimately, each individual has total control over his or her purchasing power."[5] The resource Idriss Aberkane is speaking of is knowledge. Where oil was the principal resource of the previous industrial revolution, knowledge is now at the base of today's turning point. It is not oil that we need, but knowledge to imagine new sharing platforms, open web stores or develop artificial intelligence. Consequently, a fundamental shift will occur within the economy, because unlike traditional raw materials, we can't run out of knowledge. It's an inexhaustible resource that will never dry up. "Fire is the perfect example of an economy of knowledge. I can share it, without losing it and I can multiply it without exhausting it. Even if the economy of knowledge has been around forever, today it is experiencing an acceleration, facilitated by new technologies. Today we are facing a historical turning point, similar to the Renaissance," says Idriss Aberkane.[6] We are combining an industrial revolution with a cultural revolution.

It's a direct consequence of the internet, which currently connects over 4 billion individuals. All these people are able to communicate with each other from every corner of the world and share knowledge on such an unprecedented scale that knowledge progresses at an exponential rate. For the first time ever, we're living in an economy where enrichment is made possible by sharing something. So, by sharing my knowledge with the readers of this book, they now have access to the same knowledge as I do. Sharing knowledge enables us to develop new perspectives together, which will take each one of us one step further. Compare this to the transactions during the previous industrial revolution: the seller gives oil in exchange for money and the buyer has given up his money, but has received oil. The industrial economy is based on this principle, which means that it revolves around scarcity and availability. From the outset it diminishes the possibilities of growth: an economy can't grow when it depends solely on available resources. "Infinite growth is impossible with finite resources, but infinite growth with knowledge isn't only possible, it's easy," argues Idriss Aberkane in his essay.

Knowledge as a basic resource not only enables endless growth, but also provides more equality in a certain way. We live in an era where everyone comes into this world with more or less the same starting capital: we have all received a set of neurons and thanks to the internet we all have access to the same information. Hence, we are less dependent on money, but time acquires a lot more value. To carry out a simple financial transaction, only money is required. A bank transfer just takes a split second, while transmitting knowledge takes a lot of time. This is why Idriss Aberkane doesn't think it's that bad to be (temporarily) unemployed: it offers time to increase one's level of knowledge, creating value for oneself.

Why isn't this good news on the front page?

Technological progress and the knowledge economy open up a wide range of possibilities. We are on the verge of resolving big global issues thanks to technology, while our current obsession with money must make way for another kind of wealth: the exchange of knowledge between individuals. And yet we seem to be convinced that the world is at its worst. This can be explained by the fact that the two evolutions create important changes in the economy and, by extension, in the whole of society. The world is changing at a rapid pace that we weren't prepared for. The digital revolution, this new industrial revolution we are currently experiencing is, by definition, a very turbulent period, because according to the concept developed by Austrian economist Joseph Schumpeter, each industrial revolution is linked to creative destruction. Creative destruction indicates the continuous process of innovation where new technologies eliminate the old and where new businesses overthrow well-established companies. Economist Peter de Keyzer[7] declares: "If companies didn't disappear, our economy would become petrified and we would still be working in the mines." On the one hand, creative destruction allows well-being to continue growing, but on the other hand it creates great turmoil, which brings about fear and uncertainty.

Several physical phenomena explain our incapacity to overcome this anxiety. Most of it is due to our prehistoric brains, as they are programmed to rapidly detect danger. Fear derives from a strong survival instinct. Hunters who didn't inspect the hunting area for possible dangers, would quickly become prey themselves. Instinctively, humans attach greater importance to danger than to new windows of opportunity. In addition, technology is currently developing so fast that we are overwhelmed by one anxiety-provoking factor after another without ever having time to catch our breath. "We are interpreting a global world with a system built for local landscapes. And because we've never seen it be-

Our current obsession with money must make way for another kind of wealth: the exchange of knowledge between individuals.

fore, exponential change makes even less sense. [...] Technologies are exploding and conjoining like never before, and our brains can't easily anticipate such rapid transformation. [...] This presents us with a fundamental psychological problem. Abundance is a global vision built on the backbone of exponential change, but our local and linear brains are blind to the possibility, the opportunities it may present, and the speed at which it will arrive," claim Peter Diamandis and Steven Kotler in *Abundance*.[8]

Some even believe that the human being is not capable of dealing with rapid change and that the technological evolution is beyond our capacity to adapt, causing all kinds of illnesses, such as mental breakdowns. But humanity has already undergone similar processes: during the first half of the 20th century our grandparents experienced things, like the advent of automobiles, planes, telephones and the two world wars, which were much more radical than those we have to deal with.

According to professor Steven Pinker of Harvard University, three psychological prejudices would lead us to believe that the world is a much darker place than it really is. First, a negative event lasts longer than a positive event. Chances are that the memory of losing money will last longer than the memory of gaining money. On top of that, we consider critics (who, by definition, deliver negative messages) to be engaged people. When invoking problems, they send out a signal of caring for others and naturally we feel attracted by these negativists. The third prejudice is based on nostalgia for a bygone era, a time when everything seemed simpler and better than it is today. Regardless of the era we live in and independent of our degree of wellbeing, we continue to think that times were better before.[9]

Also, Daniel Kahneman, Israeli psychologist and Nobel prize winner, points out that people don't evaluate the probability of an event based on facts, but based on how easy it is to find examples. The more notable an event is, the higher we estimate the chances of it happening. A press release about lower crime rates will go unnoticed but the story of an intruder who killed an entire family will attract attention and will make us think it can happen to us. In the same way, widely reported layoffs lodge in our brains, making us believe that our turn will come, sooner or later. Even if the newspapers tell us that an increasing number of jobs are being created. It's easier for us to remember notable events because they're reported a lot more. To give a typical example: people are more afraid of getting on a plane than in a car. And yet, the risk of being killed in a car accident much higher, but a plane crash is more spectacular and will get international media attention. The fact that more people die in car accidents in one day than in plane-related accidents in one year hardly interests the media.

All these elements converge in the way we consume information and the way media affects us. The main focus is on negative events, reinforcing the impression that we live in a world where things are bad and getting worse. Economist Max Roser of Oxford University[10] writes: "I do not think that the media are the only ones to blame, but I do think that they are to blame for some part of this. This is because the media does not tell us how the world is changing, it tells us what in the world goes wrong. One reason why the media focuses on things that go wrong is that the media focuses on single events and single events are often bad — look at the news: plane crashes, terrorism attacks, natural disasters, election outcomes that we are not happy with. Positive developments on the other hand often happen very slowly and never make the headlines in the event-obsessed media."

A new international movement is arguing in favor of constructive journalism intended to give the media another role. Ulrik Haagerup is one of the principal initiators. This former director of Danish public television speaks out against sensationalistic journalism in his book *Constructive News*. "It is time to get out of the straightjacket that the tabloids have put on even the so-called serious media. The focus of the yellow press on dallying entertainment, postulating drama, simplistic conflicts, haunt on everybody with power, and the claim to be the true defender against the evil system has for years been the key to success in the media industry. […] which also became the concept for TV news: make it short, make it uncomplicated, make it fast, make it dramatic and undifferentiated, so that the conflict is clear."[11]

Things have never been better

When we live in fear of new technologies and their impact on society, we lose sight of the progress already made in the past centuries. This progress would never have been possible without continuous technological innovation. Even if populist parties convey a different message, things have never been better. It's the postulate of Swedish economist and historian Johan Norberg global bestseller *Progress: Ten Reasons to Look Forward to the Future*. Supported by a vast amount of data, issued by the World Bank, the World Health Organization, and the United Nations, the author establishes that the world has never been a safer and healthier place to live. Famine is no longer an issue in Europe, as was the case up until the 19th century. Not too long ago, half of the world's population suffered from chronic malnutrition, compared to the current 10%. Improved health conditions, drinking water, and medical progress have paved the way to a monumental increase in average life expectancy. In 1800, the average age was limited to 40; today, even in the poorest countries it's the lowest. Peter Adamson, a UNICEF consultant, commented on the demographic explosion: "It's not that we've suddenly started breeding like rabbits; it's just that we've stopped dying like flies." Wellbeing has increased and, over the last 25 years, every day 138,000 people step away from the threshold of extreme poverty. Literacy projects, improved education and the spread of democracy have contributed to more tolerance. About one hundred years ago, women had no right to vote, anywhere. Today, the battle for women's rights is on every agenda. The world has also become a less violent place. Wars are less frequent and destructive than they were in the last generation. That probably doesn't seem so obvious when you open a newspaper or turn on the radio, but statistically it lines up.

In addition, a large part of our current economic progress isn't measured. For example, almost everyone owns a smartphone, which costs relatively little, especially when considering that all its features make it unnecessary to purchase a separate GSM, GPS, camera, personal organizer, calculator, mp3 player, encyclopedia, and a game console.

The smartphone makes it unnecessary to purchase a separate GSM, GPS, camera, personal organizer, calculator, mp3 player, encyclopedia, and a game console.

Because it replaces all these devices, the smartphone allows us to save a fair amount of money. However, there are no economic calculations taking this into consideration. The same is true of the online encyclopedia, Wikipedia. For the first time in history, everybody has free access to a very complete encyclopedia without having to invest in an expensive set of printed books.

So, digitalization has enriched us over the last few years, without us being able to really measure this prosperity. This can be explained by the fact that wellbeing is evaluated by the gross domestic product (GDP), in other words the global value of all products and services we produce. The inventor of the GDP, American economist Simon Kuznets, declared in 1934: "A nation's welfare can scarcely be inferred from their national income." This problem has become even more acute since digitalization. The quality of numerous products and services has increased exponentially in the last few years, but the GDP doesn't take this into account. In addition, the digital economy offers, free of charge, a number of products and services not included in the GDP measurements. In other words, even if digital technologies are hardly visible in economic statistics, they have an obvious positive impact on our lives.

Income inequalities

Unfortunately, these encouraging aspects are largely rendered invisible by the predominance of the emphasis placed on income inequalities. This can be partially explained by the way the success of big technology companies, and their now multibillionaire founders, is perceived. Some will say that the digital economy follows the principle of *winner takes all*. The most popular platforms become leading platforms barring the way to other potential winners. A small number of companies generate mega benefits and by doing so they create a small, closed circle of tremendously rich people. Often, the same principle is projected on the whole of society. Don't get me wrong: I don't deny that income inequalities exist. When French economist Thomas Piketty published his book *Capital in the Twenty-First Century* in 2013, it rapidly became a bestseller and the author became a leading figure in the battle against income inequality. He affirms in his book that if these inequalities have become greater over the last few years, it is because returns on capital (benefits, interest and rental income) have increased faster than economic growth. In short, it means that capitalists get richer, while the working class gains less.

A year earlier, economist Branko Milanovic also analyzed income inequalities in a report issued by the World Bank. It includes a chart reflecting changes in global income between 1988 and 2008. The horizontal axis represents the income percentile from poor to rich and the vertical axis represents the income change. With a bit of imagination, we can see the lines of the graph look like the contours of an elephant: the curve soars up (lower incomes grew strongly on a global level), then takes a plunge (lower middle class hardly experienced any change in income in the western world) and then, the curve takes off again (like the poor, the richest see their income grow strongly between 1988 and 2008). This elephant graph made it around the world. However, it's not that easy to compare different income percentiles from different eras, so Branko Milanovic has

Elephant curve

Increase in real income*, 1988-2008, %

By percentile of global income distribution

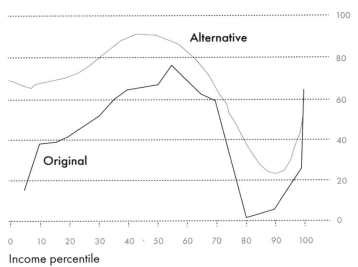

*At purchasing power parity   Source: Christoph Lakner & Branko Milanovic, World Bank

revised his original graph somewhat. This alternative graph didn't capture as much attention though. We can still make out the elephant, but the income inequalities are less pronounced and lower middle class has gained (but to be clear, still less than the poor and the rich).[12] So we all progress and the most impoverished people experience more change than the middle class. The poorest represent a huge group and they are the ones who most need an increase in income. It's not a problem in itself if a small group of already rich people becomes even richer, but it's important to keep on improving distribution.

Belgium serves as an international example when it comes to income inequalities. This stems from research done at the end of 2017 by KU Leuven (Catholic University of Leuven) economist André Decoster. The gap between the rich and the poor has closed faster in Belgium than in most other countries. If approximately 9.2% of all income was flowing towards the richest 1% in 1990, their part in 2013 had diminished to 8.3%.[13] This increase is due to the redistribution methods of the Belgian tax system: I wouldn't want to live in a country where those with fewer opportunities had to live on the street while others were able to live in luxury. These situations really exist in the world. Such inequalities are increasingly noticeable in the United States, where they have returned to the same level as they were in the years leading up to the First World War. The result is that the middle class is worried. They've lost their jobs to computerization and to industrial decline and find themselves with their backs to the wall. When they haven't got much more to lose, people turn to extreme personalities who convey populist messages.

I don't want to pretend that income inequality doesn't exist, but I want to put them in the right perspective. To start with, it's wrong to say that the digital and internet industries have suddenly created an extravagant number of billionaires. Of course, they exist. Jeff Bezos, the man behind Amazon, was declared the "Richest Man in the World" by Forbes in 2018.[14] But, the top 100 counts only about fifteen people whose fortune is derived from computing and the internet. Plus, I don't really care that there are super rich people in the world, especially if their fortune comes from innovation and entrepreneurial spirit rather than a petroleum empire. Mostly, we need to make sure that everyone has the opportunity to move forward. The consequence of putting the emphasis on income inequality is that we are obsessed by the incomes of the rich. However, that is not all there is to say about (in)equality in the world. Equality also relates to wellbeing, access to quality education, happiness and security. Our ambition should be to provide more equality and I'm intentionally not mentioning income equality. This is the very essence of seeing to it that each of us is allowed the same starting opportunities in an increasingly global and digital world.

CHAPTER 2

The history
of the future

Robots seize control of worker's jobs and intelligent computers replace employees. In other words, everyone is out of a job. This is the worst-case scenario that feeds the fears of a lot of people when it comes to the digital revolution. However, the previous industrial revolutions have also caused profound changes in the economy and society as a whole. Those changes were no less radical than the ones of the current digital revolution.

Modern Times - Charlie Chaplin

The first industrial revolution started around 1750 in England and brought us the high-pressure steam engine. It involved a motorized force that reduced the need for the strength and energy provided by human muscle, horses, water and wind. Miners were able to descend deeper than ever. Steam-powered weaving looms created a textile industry capable of mass production at lower prices. The industrial revolution then spread to the rest of the economy. Big cities were connected by railway lines and the train became a masterpiece of technology that inspired great fear. Society changed profoundly: a new category of workers came into being and wellbeing grew, unfortunately at the expense of much of the working class.

The second industrial revolution started during the second half of the 19th century and lasted until the First World War. Electricity, a new source of energy, allowed assembly lines to be implemented in factories, contributing to mass production. The telegraph, followed by the telephone, introduced a new way of communicating and the invention of the internal combustion engine was followed by automobiles in the streets. Steel was a very important raw material and cities were connected to water and gas networks, considerably improving the quality of life. "The importance of the second industrial revolution inventions was such that it took up to one hundred years for the effect to be fully experienced. Their influence was even prolonged into the 1970s, with innovations like color television, air-conditioning and the construction of an extensive road network,"[15] writes economist Koen De Leus in *Winners Economy*.

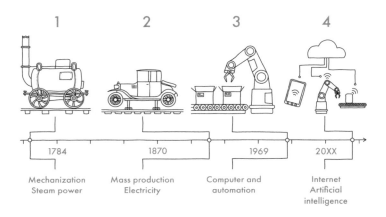

Robots take over tasks, not jobs

In retrospect, we can only affirm that the first two industrial revolutions profoundly changed the world by improving it. New technologies that were developed then have created a new economy that has helped in the development of our current wellbeing, despite the fact that they provoked great uncertainty at the time. The big problem that technological innovation has to deal with is the difficulty of imagining the form it will take and what new jobs it will create. A lot of professions have disappeared, the coachman for instance. But we needed train drivers, truck drivers and, later on, airplane pilots. At the start of the industrial revolutions, no one would ever have imagined the existence of trains, trucks and planes. Therefore, no one could have predicted that workers would one day be needed to pilot these vehicles. As long as air travel didn't exist, who would have imagined "flight attendant" as a profession? It's that same mechanism that generates anxiety today.

However, a lot of people predict that we are headed inexorably towards mass unemployment and the decline of our society. "Even if the technology doesn't cause broadscale unemployment, it can

As long as air travel didn't exist, who would have imagined "flight attendant" as a profession?

result in major problems like the rise of inequality and stagnating wages. Also, this wave of automation represents a greater threat than we've experienced in the past."[16] This is how Ryan Avent, journalist for the famous weekly magazine *The Economist* and author of a book on the consequences of technology on employment, pictures our future. The American historian James Livingston even goes so far as to claim: "No net jobs have been created in the United States since the year 2000. In certain European countries, unemployment has reached the highest point ever. The arrival of robots is only going to make things worse."[17]

Media reports are full of catastrophic scenarios like this and it should come as no surprise that a lot of people worry about the digital revolution and fear for their jobs. But, is there a real basis to this fear? A McKinsey[18] study paints a much more nuanced picture. Researchers closely analyzed the economy of nine European countries, which they consider to be precursors of digitalization: Belgium, Denmark, Estonia, Finland, Ireland, Luxembourg, the Netherlands, Norway and Sweden. They found that between 1999 and 2010 each year digital technology destroyed approximately 120,000 jobs in those countries. If we continue like this, yes, indeed, our future doesn't seem so bright. But, simultaneously, digital technology has also created 200,000 new jobs, in such a way that the request for workers has increased by 80,000 jobs a year. And those new jobs aren't solely to be found in the tech sector. Nearly 80,000 of the 200,000 new jobs are tied to digital technology and the IT sector. The other 120,000 appeared in other sectors. The new technology generates a boost in productivity, resulting in a more competitive economy, more exports, job creation and increased wellbeing. More job opportunities are created in traditional professions, from the pizza delivery person to the furniture maker, while generating new job categories such as data analyst and digital publicity manager. This is how German electronics companies profited greatly from implementing robotic automation in the automobile industry and were able to create new jobs.

Too many people are obsessed by the job losses that were announced with a big bang, whereas many others were and are being created at the same time, but in deafening silence. Marc De Vos, director of the Itinera think tank, has the following to say on the subject: "Centuries of technological innovation have taught us that each new wave destroys obsolete jobs, improves others, and creates new ones. The balance of this permanent revolution is in surplus."

"In 2017, with decades of robots, computers and internet behind us, we have never reached this level of prosperity. Never were there as many people capable of building a life thanks to gainful employment. Will the future be dramatically different? Not likely. The negative predictions make the capital error of mistaking tasks and jobs. It's not because the computer is able to fulfill certain tasks for lawyers or journalists that we won't need lawyers and journalists any more. It's not because an algorithm can manage stock exchange transactions that financial advisors become useless. It's not because a software program can perform medical analysis that doctors will disappear. Progress in terms of robots and artificial intelligence won't make humans unnecessary, but they will supplement and help them in their jobs. Where jobs effectively do disappear, new jobs can be created. If an intelligent robot were to arrive in every household and every factory, a giant new sector of development, conception, construction, programming, selling, delivery and maintenance of these robots will see the day."[19]

Contrary to a widely held idea, the jobs created won't be reserved solely for highly-educated people capable of programming. The profes-

There's no chance that in 2030 a robot will come to your home to repair a leaky pipe.

sions of technician and nurse will certainly not disappear. There's no chance that in 2030 a robot will come to your home to repair a leaky pipe. Looking at it from this perspective, becoming a plumber is a future profession that will ensure job

March 1964	April 1978	September 2016
Automation in Germany. The appearance of robots.	The digital revolution. How progress kills jobs.	You're fired! How computers and robots steal our jobs and which jobs will still be here tomorrow.

Robots take over tasks, not jobs

security. But, chances are that the plumber will be able to rely on artificial intelligence to respond faster to the demand and in a more qualitative way. Traditional jobs will continue to exist in 2030, but aspects of those jobs will change. Farmers will use drones to irrigate their fields, assembly workers will have intelligent glasses that deliver instructions on how to operate a machine, and a mover will move heavy furniture with the help of an exoskeleton. And, for those whose jobs have become redundant because of technology, there is always the possibility to retrain and become a cyber-detective to address internet criminality, a robot coach to improve the artificial intelligence of machines, or to become a rescue worker and intervene from a distance using a webcam and deliver first aid while waiting for the doctor to arrive. So how is it that there will be a lack of jobs?

Democracy through digitalization

The fear of mass unemployment is only one of the numerous aspects that highlight the extent of the digital revolution. It has already deeply changed our way of living and working and there is no evidence that it will ever stop. We are only at the beginning of a new industrial revolution. Why is the digitalization wave so important? To answer this question, let's go back to the 1950s when the very first computers made their way into companies. Today, there are hardly any jobs left where information technology isn't being used. Even the plumber uses a computer or laptop to communicate with his clients, to place orders and to create invoices. Computers have taken over a huge number of tasks and increased productivity. And yet they haven't disrupted our daily lives, which explains why all economists and historians don't consider the introduction of the computer as the third industrial revolution. However, it is possible that in the future it will be considered the element that started it. Computers have been the necessary tools for digitalization, the same way oil refineries were able to deliver, from the start of the second half of the 19th century, the raw material necessary for the new round of the second industrial revolution. The true innovation appeared only when all computers could be linked together and the internet came into being. This takes us back to 1969, when the U.S. Department of Defense established the ARPANET, a network that linked different research institutions working on military projects. That year, the network connected four universities, including Stanford. Year after year, more networks connected to the ARPANET. At the end of the 1980s, it lost its military function and was abolished, but the foundation for the internet had been laid. There was still one more difficulty to overcome. A network such as the ARPANET wasn't accessible to the public. It was impossible to make further headway without knowledge of the protocol. Moreover, a graphical interface was nonexistent and the exchange of information consisted only of texts. But all of this changed when British Tim Berners-Lee and Belgian Robert Cailliau introduced the World Wide Web in 1989. Access to information became fairly easy with the help of user-friendly web browsers, while hyperlinks made it simple to click from one page to another. The internet, as we know it today, was born.

The World Wide Web has changed our lives a great deal more than the computer has. Never before had we been given access to so much information. And, it was available for anyone to consult. The days of bulky and expensive encyclopedias are not that far behind us. That was before the online encyclopedia Wikipedia completely replaced them. By doing so, Wikipedia has democratized access to knowledge: from that moment forward, everybody was given the ability to consult an encyclopedia free of charge. Also, Wikipedia is more up to date and easy to use than a traditional encyclopedia and the content is of better quality thanks to the discussion pages, cooperation and network control. Today, all you need is a smartphone to access an encyclopedia from anywhere, while just twenty years ago many people didn't hesitate to spend thousands of euros to own one, and that one was only available in your library, at home.

In addition, the internet also created a fundamental turning point: thanks to social networks, such as Facebook, we've never had so many friends. Finding old classmates is as easy as a click of the mouse, when before it took time and determination to get in contact with long-lost friends. Of course, the sincerity of Facebook friendships can be questioned, however, they emphasize the daily changes brought about by the internet and the importance of the global community that has been created. The internet has also changed our way of watching television. Computers supplemented television with subtitles and closed captioning, but we can't really say that it fundamentally changed the viewing experience. On the other hand, digitalization changed everything: now it's possible to view your favorite television program when you want and not just when it's scheduled. Newspapers also perfectly illustrate the changes that happened thanks to the internet. The arrival of computers and information technology has considerably improved the presentation of newspapers through the use of pictures and attractive layouts, but the content hasn't changed. As for digitalization, it has shaken the foundations of the sector, because the news is no longer exclusively of the written or televised press: the internet continually provides us with the latest news every minute.

All of this leads us to the real reasons that explain the importance of digitalization. It creates *dematerialization*. For example, it's no longer necessary to print encyclopedias or newspapers. Which leads to *demonetization*: if it's expensive to print and distribute paper newspapers, broadcasting of digital information requires fewer variable costs. Consequently, *democratization* becomes possible, as information is available at an insignificant cost for everyone.

The smartphone revolution

It took decades for the big mainframe computers to become personal computers and another decade for those PC's to become part of our daily lives. In the past, it was enough to be a little bit interested in innovation to be able to follow the technological evolutions without much difficulty. Today, that's no longer the case. The mobile internet has given a big boost to digitalization. The internet from the beginning maybe triggered a revolution, but is still had its limits: you had to sit behind your desk to connect your PC to the internet using a, sometimes very slow, modem. Surfing the internet was a conscious act, which we indulged in once a day, or week or even once a month. Today is completely different. The smartphone allows us to be permanently connected and often we are hardly aware of being online. And that's precisely where the challenge of technology lies: it has to work in the background for you; the technical manipulations should not hinder the user-friendliness and everything should go without saying. Smartphone users use their devices an average of 150 times a day.[20] It's as normal to have internet access at home as it is to have electricity. Anyone who owns a smartphone today has access to more information than the President of the United States had ten years ago. The effect on society is tremendous. Political regimes can be put under pressure and citizens

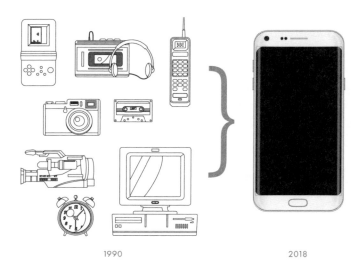

1990   2018

The smartphone became a real jack-of-all-trades.

can take power. Access to the web should be a fundamental right for all humans. The web opens us up to free information, online education, medical information, and to culture.

The breakthrough of mobile internet coincides with the launch of the first Apple iPhone in 2007, making smartphones accessible to the public. Does this mean that Apple invented the smartphone? Not at all. Blackberry smartphones were already really popular when the iPhone first arrived, but they were mostly used by business people. Apple's technology was by no means revolutionary, but this giant managed to develop a device that was significantly better in terms of design and user friend-liness. So, it took the iPhone for the larger public to be ready for mobile internet and to take total ownership of the smartphone. In the meantime, mobile internet became ubiquitous to the point where it absorbed all other devices.

When the internet first started, everyone used a travel planner on their computers to set-up an itinerary, while also keeping a GPS in the car. We took pictures with a digital camera, transferred the pictures to our PC or laptop and shared them on the internet. And today? The smartphone has become a window to the world and has replaced an entire series of devices. Wherever we go, we use it as a GPS, a camera to take pictures and share them instantly with the rest of the world, an electronic agenda, a screen to watch movies or TV series on the train or on the plane and, of course, when we have a bit of free time, we use it to read the news or update our Facebook status. Even phone calls are made more often on smartphones through the internet thanks to applications such as Skype and WhatsApp. In other words, you're holding in your hand a computer that's even more powerful than the supercomputers that took up a whole room only a few decades ago.

The whole of the computing capacity in a cloud

All these new applications require an enormous amount of computing capacity and memory storage space. Countless data centers work within the internet. By itself, Google has 15 of them spread across the world in order to continue providing its services. Data centers are highly-secure buildings that house a great number of computers. This is the beating heart of the digital revolution. During the second industrial revolution, all innovations were supported by electricity. In our knowledge society, the new raw material is information and it has to go through complicated calculations performed by the data centers. When you initiate a search on your smartphone, it goes directly to a data center, which sends the results of the research to your device. Also, personal preferences are literally dealt with in a fraction of a second by this enormous computing capacity: in less than 200 milliseconds to be precise.

In the past, every company had its own data center or at least its own server. That was extremely expensive, considering that new applications require more computing power and therefore need bigger data centers. For most companies it means a big investment, not counting the fact that they don't always have access to the appropriate expertise in house. That's why more companies resort to external businesses that supply the computing power and the memory storage capacity through the internet. It's what we call *cloud computing*. Over the last couple of years, this evolution has led to an enormous increase of capacity, to the point where no technological restrictions will stop our ambitions. We now have access to an almost unlimited memory space and computing capacity. Without even knowing it, most of us have completely adopted the cloud. Let's see how we manage our digital photos. Not too long ago, we took our pictures with a digital camera, until the memory card was full. Then, you either had to erase some of them or, even better, transfer them to your PC or laptop. Today, we simply save our pictures, taken with our smartphones, in the photo application of our choice. And where does this application store all those pictures? In the cloud that hovers over the internet. That's why we are able to take an infinite number of pictures given the fact that we are no longer limited by the storage capacity of our smartphones. And if your smartphone breaks down, there's no need to get upset over lost pictures of your holiday or the newborn baby. All of your pictures are safely stored in the cloud and all you need is an internet connection and another device to recover them. It can't get any easier than this!

Computers are getting smarter

Just like the consumers who benefit from the practically infinite storage capacity of the cloud, companies also have relatively easy and less expensive access to an unprecedented computing power and digital storage capacity. This has enabled the development of machine learning and artificial intelligence, two recent phenomena closely related to one another. Machine learning consists of programming a computer in a way that makes it able to become more intelligent on its own based on the data. The computer learns all by itself, making it intelligent in some way. We call this artificial intelligence. It's not difficult to program a computer to turn on the heating when the temperature falls below a predefined level. It's different when you program a computer to only pick the photos with a dog from among all your family photos. The concept of a dog is not easy for a computer: there are different breeds of dog, they aren't all the same color or the same size, and they can appear in different positions in the photos: lying down, sitting, standing or in movement. Despite the difficulties, today it is possible for a computer to accomplish this task. A huge database has been used to make it so. Based on pixel templates, the computer tried to recognize the dogs. The result of the first trial was pathetic, but a human being then indicated in which photos dogs appeared. The computer used this information to improve its analysis and recognition of templates. Each time the task was performed it became more intelligent until it was perfectly capable of picking the right photos. The result? The computer transformed itself into a machine with artificial intelligence.

In recent decades, artificial intelligence has become the Holy Grail of computer scientists who started working on the issue from the mid-1950s forward, without being able to find the answer to their high expectations. During the 1960s, this line of research was still considered futurist and one from which concrete applications would be a long time coming. The reason being simple: scientists of that era didn't have the necessary computing power to create artificial intelligence, nor did they have significant volumes of digital data to learn from. Now we do and that's in large part due to Moore's law, named after one of the founders of the Intel chip, Gordon Moore. He predicted in 1965 that the number of chip transistors would double each year, in order for computing power to double at the same pace. Ten years later he revised his expectations to a doubling once every two years, which was still phenomenal. In any case, computing power has increased exponentially over the past few decades. It's no coincidence that Albert Einstein is said to have remarked that compound interest (exponential growth) was the eighth wonder of the world, because fabulous numbers have been reached at a rapid pace. For example: if you take 30 steps, you take a walk of approximately 30 meters. If you take 30 exponential steps, you travel around the world 26 times. It is therefore particularly complicated to represent the significance of exponential growth.

The first major milestone of artificial intelligence was set in 1997. The whole world watched in amazement as Deep Blue, IBM's supercomputer, defeated Garry Kasparov, who was the world chess champion. Computer engineers and chess experts joined forces to program Deep Blue. Basically, they ensured the computer's ability to break through the limits of the chess game by simulating every possible move until the last move and therefore arrive at the best winning strategy. The Deep Blue victory is of great symbolic importance, because it was the first time that a computer managed to beat a human being, in a strategic game based on human intelligence. The computing power of Deep Blue was impressive, but it wasn't really machine learning yet.

Another milestone was reached in 2016, when the program created by DeepMind, a British company specialized in artificial intelligence and a branch of Alphabet (Google's parent company), won against one of the best Go players in the world. Go is a Chinese game that's like chess; it's played on a square board with a 19-line grid. One player has the white stones, the other plays with the black stones. One at a time, each player puts a stone on one of the grid's intersections and tries to surround his opponent's stones with his own. The game of Go is much more complicated than chess and has more possible moves than there are atoms in the universe. Therefore, it didn't make any sense to program all possible moves, as was done for the chess game.

That is why the DeepMind engineers took a different track and experimented with machine learning. The fact that Go is very popular in Asia was an advantage; there are numerous games to watch on the internet, amateur as well as professional. All these games are real treasure troves of information, which the computer can analyze. And, while playing against a human being, the computer learns which strategies work and which don't. The real leap forward occurs when two computers play against one another. They improve their algorithms based on games lost and won. This is not about just a few games, but millions of games against one another. Then, when the computer has to face a human being, it quickly takes the upper hand, even when it plays against one of the best players in the world. Not because it's able to calculate all possible moves (that's impossible with Go), but because it uses some sort of intuition. That's the real revolution of machine learning.

Will computers become
more intelligent than humans?

It's fun that a computer program is able to beat a human being at a very complex game, but that doesn't change the world. Really? Deep Blue had been programmed to learn how to play chess and that was its only application. With DeepMind, the time had come to find new applications. For Google, machine learning has resulted in a 40% reduction in the power consumption necessary for cooling, the most energy-consuming aspect of a data center. "We managed to do so by collecting the data of thousands of sensors in a data center. We're talking about temperature, power, pump speeds and more. They are used to train an ensemble of several forms of artificial intelligence with the objective of improving the energy efficiency of the data centers,"[21] explains DeepMind.

This same technology has been used to develop a smart search function in Google's photo application: the search engine can easily extract all your winter sports photos simply based on images. And the translation application Google Translate has improved a lot thanks to machine learning. Translations that were delivered previously were mostly awkward. Today the translations come close to the work of a professional translator. For now, that is mostly valid for the most frequently used languages, such as English or Spanish, simply because more comparative information is available. Mail servers have also become more intelligent and now have a better automatic recognition of spam mail than ever before.

It's evident that no form of artificial intelligence thinks completely by itself. And even more than huge computing power, the power required by artificial intelligence is human creativity, because humans supply the information and invent the applications. Make no mistake: artificial intelligence isn't immune to stupidity. An intelligent computer can play a world-class game of chess, but when your house is on fire, it will simply continue playing chess. However, maybe someday computers will be just as intelligent as humans.

Well-known futurologist Ray Kurzweil even predicts that this will be the case in 2029. And by 2045, this technology thinker believes we will be talking about technological "singularity", which means that some sort of artificial intelligence will enable such an unprecedented technological evolution that it will change the world radically, more than could ever be done by humans. It goes without saying that computers and robots will rule the world. Ray Kurzweil wrote about this prediction for the first time in 2005, in his book *The Singularity is Near*.[22]

An intelligent computer can play a world-class game of chess, but when your house is on fire, it will simply continue playing chess.

Personally, I am skeptical about the subject. Humans are very complex beings. It's one thing to grasp the complexity of the game of Go, it's a different one to penetrate deeply into all aspects of humanity. Besides, in the past, a great number of technological innovations haven't developed by following an exponential curve. Evolution often accelerates at a given time and then eventually stabilizes. And, even if the predictions for 2029 and 2045 prove to be true, we shouldn't fear what's coming. Above all, it is important to think of ways to use and control these new

"Any time you work with technology, you need learn to harness the benefits while minimizing the downsides."

technologies in the coming years. As Google's CEO Sundar Pichai declared during the World Economic Forum in Davos in 2018: "Any time you work with technology, you need to learn to harness the benefits while minimizing the downsides."[23] This is what we've done, throughout history, every time there's a new technological innovation.

We've also often made mistakes: from the outset, we have used carbon and the automobile on a large scale. Only later did we start thinking about the environmental impact. In this regard, we've evolved. We're identifying and discussing the dangers of artificial intelligence at the beginning of developing the technology.

Nevertheless, it's clear that the current digital revolution, that combines an industrial revolution and a cultural revolution, deeply changes our world and turns it upside down. That's why a lot of people talk about "disruption": the technological revolution disrupts the Old World and tears it apart. Some even talk of "uberization", making an analogy with the introduction of Uber, which has supposedly driven traditional taxis out of business. Meanwhile, we know that traditional taxis coexist with Uber, but this transformation is still experienced as negative.

As far as I'm concerned, I prefer the word "reinvention". We have to rethink the world in the light of available technology. The second part of this book analyzes the impact on different aspects of our society. It includes for example health care, education, or shopping. All of these aspects of society in Digitalis will be closely monitored to try to determine how they can (or have to) be reinvented. Of course, I am not an expert in all fields, but I hope to inspire and spark ideas about the changes that we can expect to happen.

We have to reinvent the world in the light of available technology.

46

Part 2 _____ Reinventing
the world

CHAPTER 3

Defeating death

How do we reinvent healthcare?

According to Alphabet, Google's parent company, technology makes it possible to solve big problems. In 2013, Alphabet founded its own research and development company for health technology: Calico; its mission is to defeat death. I don't know if one day this will happen, but the digital revolution has all it takes to become a trump card in future healthcare policies. Artificial intelligence allows for a faster and more precise diagnosis; robots improve the chances of successful surgery; and new measurement devices (including chips placed in our own bodies) will be of great help to doctors to identify illnesses or fatal conditions at a much earlier stage. First and foremost, this technology will save a lot of lives and will keep people in better health and for a longer period of time. At the same time, healthcare will gain efficiency, offering the best guarantee for preserving the European social system. However, costs are very high, which explains why healthcare is under pressure. Economies can guarantee access, but quality can be compromised. And in the meantime, costs continue to go up due to the fact that an increasing number of people need

This is where digitalization offers a solution.

medical attention not only because of demographic growth, but also because of the ageing population. This is where digitalization offers a solution. If, in a way, it can provide added value, it is possible that product or service prices will be significantly reduced, while quality and accessibility improve.

When patients become clients

Last year, my daughter had foot surgery. Everything went well: she received excellent medical attention and the amount we had to pay out of pocket was relatively limited. And yet, we felt some unease at certain moments. As soon as we walked into the hospital we felt like the system did not take us seriously. At times, we had to wait several hours without receiving any information. I remember one particular follow-up visit. We arrived on time, but the doctor only saw us three hours later. The doctor had a morning surgery that presented complications and took longer than planned. It's understandable and kudos to the doctor who is very serious about patient care. But the fact remains that clearly all other visits planned for that day would be postponed and that the waiting patients should have been advised. It didn't happen and it's very unpleasant to be treated this way in the 21st century. It also shows that the medical world still doesn't consider patients as clients. The analogy between the words "patient" and "patience" might not be a coincidence. In the industrial era this was unavoidable, but now that we're living in a digital world, we want to be treated as clients. Technology makes it possible. The consumer can already experience it in other areas of society where digital services are highly customized. A simple application to inform you that your medical visit has been postponed to a reasonable delay or to plan a new visit is entirely feasible without even resorting to state-of-the-art technology.

In the short term, digitalization can also serve to considerably simplify all medical paperwork. It's mind-boggling to see how many cards we still need to carry and how many forms we need to complete prior to being reimbursed for the medical examination or treatment in most European countries. This administrative merry-go-round is still based on the last century's operational methods. Many medical institutions rely on very outdated IT systems and all patient data can only be used locally. Yet, digitalization can solve all this hassle on very short notice. It would also allow doctors, and the nursing staff, to spend more time with their patients, or rather, clients.

Smarter than a doctor

Digitalization not only improves the services provided, artificial intelligence also allows diagnostics to be more precise. The advantage of the connectedness of 4 billion humans on the internet is that a lot more medical data is available: from innovative studies available online to patient data rendered anonymous. All these data may be used for machine learning to develop some kind of artificial intelligence capable of diagnosing or at least of offering support to doctors in this regard. Up until now, doctors could rely solely on cases they'd been taught or that they'd encountered during their working careers, but artificial intelligence can easily consider hundreds of thousands, even millions of cases and continually improve thanks to machine learning.

And I'm not talking about the distant future. Just think of Watson, IBM's supercomputer. In 2011, it participated in the

American television game show *Jeopardy!* and made the news worldwide when it played against two champions of the game...

and won! It was a major milestone in artificial intelligence: not only did Watson need to understand the spoken language, it also needed to capture irony and word play. After this performance, IBM changed its supercomputer into Dr. Watson, to use this technology for medical re-

The advantage of the connectedness of 4 billion humans on the internet is that a lot more medical data is available: from innovative studies available online to patient data rendered anonymous.

search. Over the last few years, the computer has processed thousands of pages on cancer research, as well as a variety of patient data. Therefore, technology is now capable of accompanying doctors in the treatment of some of the most common types of cancer. Its development is, however, a lot more complicated than IBM planned and it's still difficult to market. But the potential is real.

Other technology companies also focus on the healthcare sector. For example, Google has developed, aided by a vast amount of data analysis and machine learning, an algorithm for diagnosing diabetic retinopathy. You might have never heard of it, but this eye condition is one of the fastest-growing causes of blindness: globally, nearly 415 million diabetics risk experiencing this complication. An early diagnosis allows for successful treatment of the condition, but if treatment comes too late, it can cause permanent vision loss. Google researchers confirm: "Numerous parts of the world are affected by diabetes and, unfortunately, don't have access to medical specialists capable of detecting the disease. We believe that machine learning can help doctors in the identification of patients in need, especially among underprivileged populations."[24] In cooperation with doctors from India and the United States they collected some 128,000 medical images of eyes. Each image was evaluated by a specialized ophthalmologist who had to determine if it represented an affected eye and to what degree the condition was present. This gathering of data made the creation of a neuronal network, capable of recognizing the condition, possible. In the long run, artificial intelligence reduces the number of people likely to become blind and the technique is already being used at eye clinics in India.[25]

This kind of medical screening method, based on artificial intelligence, can have a significant impact on healthcare. Inaccuracies can be avoided, as well as misdiagnosis, and patients being sent from one doctor to another. Also, if it takes too long to arrive at a correct diagnosis, it often happens that the patient needs to undergo a more intensive (and more expensive) treatment or, even worse, the patient's affection is no longer treatable. Obviously, this is bad news for the patient, but it also presents a problem in terms of healthcare accessibility. When medicine is backed up by artificial intelligence, unnecessary patient suffering can be avoided and healthcare costs can be reduced.

New DNA
for medical prescription

Artificial intelligence is also a big player in the development of genetic analysis. DeepVariant is a good example. This tool has been developed by Google Brain and Verily Life Sciences. Google Brain is Google's research project dedicated to artificial intelligence and Verily Life Science is a company specialized in life science research. The objective is to try and map genetic material in greater detail using the latest artificial intelligence techniques. The human genome is like a huge playground for artificial intelligence, full of billions of information blocks. The following comparison was made by research and popular scientist Jente Ottenburghs to describe the challenge of genetics: "We can compare the genome to a big book written with the DNA alphabet, which is composed of four letters: A, T, G and C. Chromosomes are the chapters and genes form the words. Phrases without meaning have found their way in between functional genes, it's as if a cat walked on the keyboard while the book was being written. The objective of geneticists is to put all the words in the right places. And then, each paragraph has to be associated to the right chapter (chromosome). This wouldn't seem so complicated if it weren't for the fact that where human genomes are concerned, the text numbers some 3 billion letters. Or, approximately one million pages."[26]

Decoding the human genome could significantly modify healthcare, because the doctor would no longer have to try to recognize diseases based on their symptoms and then try and find the best possible cure while setting up the most efficient treatment protocol. Thanks to genetic analysis, the doctor would be able to have a look directly into your "software program" and have an easier time spotting the error. And once the error in the genome is spotted, the doctor would know exactly which disease he or she needs to deal with. Better yet, by correcting DNA errors, perhaps medicine would be able to eradicate genetic diseases. A futurist prediction? Not at all. Hordes of scientists worldwide are working on the development of genetic therapy. Among promising techniques, CRISPR is worth mentioning. Mostly it's a cut-paste function for DNA that, in the hands of geneticists, forms a powerful molecular tool for rewriting the human genetic code. Basically, it means that a new code is written where a scientist wants to replace a part of the genetic code. This new code is then associated with a protein that searches the DNA until the error code has been found. The protein cuts the DNA in half, eliminates the error code (for example, a mutation stemming from the untreatable Huntington disease) and replaces it with the scientists' corrected code. Subsequently, the DNA recovers by itself.[27]

Of course, as long as costs amounted to millions of euros, genetic analysis was not part of daily healthcare. But luckily, we've come a long way. In the year 2000, the Human Genome Project has managed for the very first time to completely map the DNA structure. Bill Clinton, then President of the United States, officially declared: "Today, we are learning the language in which God created life."[28] Scientists saw a revolutionary prediction in diagnostics, treatments and disease prevention. The Human Genome Project's started in 1990 and its final achievement wasn't until 2003. The total cost of the project reached nearly 3 billion dollars. The actual cost of the DNA decoding is estimated at from 500 million to 1 billion dollars. Since then, the price of genetic analysis has decreased at an exponential rate. In 2006, the cost of this kind of analysis was approximately 14 million dollars. By mid-2015, it didn't cost more than 4,000 dollars and by the beginning of 2016, the price had gone down to less than 1,500 dollars.[29] Today, all it takes is to send a saliva sample to a company (e.g. MyHeritage, AncestryDNA or 23andMe) to receive a genetic analysis for less than 200 dollars. Some seem to believe that the price is likely to go even lower, to only a few dollars. Everybody would be able to request a genetic analysis. We'll be able to find out whether practicing sports intensively is good for us, what our risks are of getting a disease, and which foods we need to avoid.

Microchips in our bodies

Other than artificial intelligence, new possibilities are also being created with microelectronics. Most people have their blood pressure measured when they go the doctor, more or less once or twice a year. No one is able to tell what occurs in between those occasional medical visits. It wouldn't, however, be an unnecessary luxury to measure blood pressure on a regular basis, if it were only so that we could be aware of high blood pressure, which increases the danger of cardiovascular disease. It's the same with the heart rate: for no particular reason, the doctor will occasionally check it. In a near future, we won't be checking on our health in these outdated and random ways. With the latest microelectronic evolutions, we will be able to continually measure our health status with smartphone applications, body sensors and implants. The trendiest and most tangible example today is Fitbit. This intelligent sports watch measures your heart beat, counts your steps, checks the number of calories burned, calculates your speed and monitors your sleep. Small devices can measure and register everything in a way that allows the doctor to notify us when we are going in the wrong direction. The continuous monitoring helps doctors to make an earlier diagnosis, which gives treatment a better chance for success. What's more, these little measurement devices aren't that expensive in comparison to the cost of the intensive treatments they may allow you to avoid. One day, applications will receive information about the burger you're eating, sensors placed on your body will measure their fat content and you'll get a notification to adapt your diet if necessary.

These harmless measuring devices will radically change over the next few years. For a while, we'll still depend on external instruments, such as bracelets, watches or patches. But things can change faster than we think. This is how the Food and Drug Administration (a federal agency in charge of pharmaceutical industry control in the United States), gave the green light in November 2017 to the launching of a digital variation to Abilify[30], medication designed for psychiatric patients. This digital medication holds an ingestible sensor that sends a signal as soon as it makes contact with gastric fluid. From that moment on, doctors can monitor whether or not their patients are taking their medication.

Google researchers and the pharmaceutical company Novartis are in the midst of developing an application to produce intelligent contact lenses for people suffering from diabetes. The lenses hold a tiny chip that's able to read the blood sugar level through tears. The lens changes colors according to the sugar level: green when it becomes necessary to eat a bit of sugar, red when it's time for an insulin injection. Today, diabetics need to prick themselves several times a day to measure their blood sugar level. Not only is it uncomfortable, but it also doesn't tell them how their blood sugar changes between the two measurements. It's like driving your car and only seeing that you've exceeded the speed limit twice a day. An intelligent lens will change all this. This technology isn't ready yet and we're a few years away from seeing it marketed, but it clearly shows the direction we're headed.

Even having a microchip in your head is no longer considered science fiction. Elon Musk, the founder of electric car brand Tesla, founded the Neuralink company, with the objective of connecting the human brain to a computer. The technology functions through brain implants with the goal of making the human brain more intelligent. Let's not forget Bryan Johnson, the American entrepreneur who earned a fortune selling his company, PayPal. He used part of his 800 million for the Kernel foundation, a company with the ambition to cure different types of neurological afflictions with the aid of brain implants. It would be an important step forward in fighting diseases such as Alzheimer's or Parkinson's.

The surgeon is a robot

Robots represent a big evolution in the medical industry. Even if the medical application of robotics is still in a very early stage, robots will eventually take over numerous surgeries normally carried out by human surgeons or, at the very least offer significant assistance. And there's nothing wrong with that, because humans aren't infallible. When you're going in for surgery, you have to put all your confidence in the surgeon and hope that he's at his best, but there's never a guarantee. In the future, a surgeon will always be present in the operating room. Computers, that direct the robots, will be preprogrammed by the surgeon who will supervise and intervene when necessary. The work of a surgeon will be less and less hands-on. Increasingly the surgeon will be supervising the surgery, as the anesthetist already does. Robots will quickly, and with increasing precision, take care of medical procedures. More surgeries can be done in less time, which will drastically reduce errors and the surgeon's exhaustion. Does it sound crazy to you? The carpenter doesn't just use his handsaw anymore either; he has automated power saws he can program to saw with even more precision. Sure, the human body is very complex, but technology is slowly developing so that it will be up for the challenge.

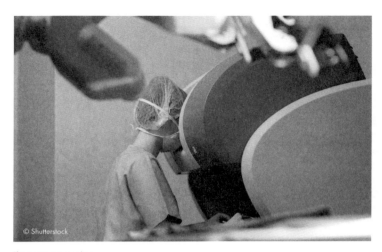
© Shutterstock

The surgeon is a robot.

Of course, it will still take time before robots will be completely independent to perform surgery and meanwhile, surgeons are increasingly using them as precision instruments. With their hands on the controllers and feet on the pedals they guide different robotized arms. This is, for example, how they can remove a kidney tumor while saving a large part of the organ. Up until now, robotic surgery has mostly been performed in the urology field; gynecologists and gastroenterologists also rely more frequently on robots. Alex Mottrie is surgeon at the hospital in Aalst (Belgium) and a world leader and pioneer in robotic surgery. He founded a training facility where surgeons from all over the world learn how to operate with robots. "In reality, we don't work with intelligent robots yet. I'm always the master and the robot is the slave. When I move, the robot imitates me and miniaturizes my movements. But stand-alone robots will arrive sooner rather than later. Robots that will be able to remove a tumor by themselves based on 3D images and all sorts of scans that will be transmitted to them; that's my dream," the surgeon says. [31]

Does this mean that there's no future for doctors? No, of course not. We'll still run into doctors in the hospital corridors. No robot and no form of artificial intelligence can replace them. But a distinction will be drawn between two types of profiles. On the one hand, certain doctors will become more technical, because they will work primarily with computer specialists, engineers and bioinformaticians in order to develop artificial intelligence, microelectronics and medical robotics. This would be an impossible task for technicians to achieve without the information and the knowledge of doctors. On the other hand, there's a need for doctors with excellent emotional intelligence. Artificial intelligence can help doctors to arrive at a diagnosis, but to entrust the delicate task of informing the patient that he or she is suffering from cancer to an algorithm is impossible. It takes a doctor to accompany the patient, to contextualize things correctly and to present the patient with possible treatment options. We'll always need doctors to interface between machines and patients. This also means that the emotional approach towards patients should be considered during medical studies, because it will be crucial for future doctors.

Deontology and privacy rights

The use of new digital technologies in the healthcare sector comes with fundamental aspects like privacy rights and deontology. There's no doubt that artificial intelligence is a powerful force for medical progress, but its intelligence is solely built on data. Without an enormous mountain of data, it would be

Medical files in Congo,
where my daughter Manon is working on a project for the Tropical Institute.

impossible to develop viable artificial intelligence applications
to improve or even save human lives. Yet, in Europe, it is not
easy to collect all the vital data needed to get to work. Scientists
have to consider the privacy of each individual. Protection of
privacy is a legitimate concern that, under no circumstances,
should be overlooked; but it shouldn't interfere with the development of innovative technologies that may save lives. A balance needs to be found. People may be prepared to share their
medical data in order to allow research to progress and participate, in a way, in their own recovery or that of others. Clearly no
one wants life insurance companies to have access to medical
records and increase insurance rates when health problems occur, or an employer who picks candidates based on their genetic

features. At the same, it has to be possible to protect confidentiality before gathering all the information in a large medical database. Not doing so would be a lack of long-term vision.

Anonymizing patient data from all hospitals would create a large medical database available for consultation, under strict conditions, by professors and researchers working in the medical sector in a broad sense, including also the pharmaceutical and biotechnological sectors. It would boost innovation in Europe. And, it's in our interest.

If our companies can no longer propose innovative solutions, others will, like Asian companies for example. They have another approach to privacy rights, as well as a different legal framework. This is why it is so important that a maximum amount of data be made available to our own companies and research centers, using a solid legal framework. Protecting our own standards and values should be the objective, but in such a way that it doesn't get in the way of innovation.

Also, a deontological debate on genetic analysis is necessary. It's a very good thing that a doctor can identify a serious heart defect by analyzing your DNA and is then able to save your life with surgery. But what happens if he's faced with a life-threatening genetic disorder he's not able to treat? What would your life be like, living each day knowing this? It's a delicate issue. I'm a great believer in genetic analysis, provided that a big enough psychological, medical and deontological filter is being used, as has been done in dealing with euthanasia. A debate is necessary: about information that should be given to the patient, because it can make the patient happier or even cure them, and about information that should be kept from the patient until the moment is right. This debate has not yet been initiated either by the medical sector or by the patients (who don't have these analyses carried out yet or who'd like to know everything). It's absolutely necessary to raise these issues, because technology is on the move. Europe could be pioneering in the matter and define the rhythm of innovation in line with our standards and values.

The American Silicon Valley massively invests in companies and young start-ups oriented towards healthcare. Traditional pharmaceutical firms have to deal with competition from a field they didn't expect. The European pharmaceutical industry has to reinvent itself again. If it can pull it off, our companies could be pioneers of the 21st century, as they've already been in the past century.

CHAPTER 4

Smart houses in smart cities

How do we reinvent
our homes and our cities?

I live in a terraced house and I like it. Our neighbors sometimes complain about the bus that runs on our street, but that was actually the reason why I chose to live here. Living in the city, instead of a rural area, makes it possible for my children to get around by themselves, by bicycle or public transport. I don't have to drive them places all the time and we've all gained a bit of freedom.

It seems that my dream house is not the same one Europeans traditionally dream of, which is good. Owning a house surrounded by green isn't possible for everybody anymore. Luckily, Digitalis offers plenty of alternative solutions. Many people dread the idea of living in a smaller house or of moving to a city or the center of town. But the principles of digital economy enable everyone to live more centrally, more efficiently and more ecologically without having to sacrifice comfort. In fact, it's just the opposite, because more luxury is available at a reasonable price. Not to mention the breakthrough of home automation, or domotics, which will improve user-friendliness. Then there are the 3D printers that will enable us to build our own house. So, I ask you this. Who wouldn't want to live in Digitalis?

A house with a swimming pool for everyone

Finding a house at an affordable price has become increasingly difficult over the last few years. First, you have to save money for a long time to pay for a part of the house; then, you spend a third of your life paying back the mortgage loan. Also, bank policies have become a lot stricter in granting mortgage loans.

Digital evolution can be the strong link to affordable housing. In many areas, digitalization has already allowed more flexibility and accessibility. The principles of digital economy allow us to move away from material possessions and to evolve towards availability. It will no longer be necessary to invest in your own car, but we can have access to one at any given time on a sharing platform. We'll no longer need to purchase music and films; they're consumed via streaming, which gives access to so much content that you'll never be able to watch or listen to it all. As for products that we use only occasionally, like tools, sharing platforms already exist. Where housing is concerned, most people still seem to be still very self-centered. Depending on the intensification of the sharing economy, this may change.

Co-housing is starting to be a success, even if it's still a marginal trend. Several families choose to live collectively or, in addition to their own house, they have shared spaces and facilities. A grouped housing complex consists, for example, of a dozen houses or apartments. While they have separate private accommodation, the families share, for example, a garden or terrace, a workshop, a recreation room or a multipurpose room with a kitchen. Such projects are based on the principles of the sharing economy: each family doesn't buy individual housing for itself, but shares their investment with others to benefit from economies of scale. We are not the sole owners of the project, but we enjoy the facilities that one family can't afford on its own. The number of grouped residences should double in the next few years.[32]

Several specialists support the housing types based on the sharing economy. One of them is master architect Leo van Broeck who argues in favor of grouped residences with small units, completed with shared spaces. For a lot of people, grouped residency and co-housing seems like the end of the dream of parceling when in reality it's the contrary. Sharing gives the opportunity to afford a level of luxury that's generally out of reach. Leo van Broeck gives an example: "There's a vegetable garden and a barbecue on the roof of the apartment building. The basement has a space to wash your mountain bike. There's also a swimming pool and a soundproof room where you can play the piano. A number of facilities that are usually only available in large houses."[33]

Nonetheless, it will take some time for everyone to sell their individual homes and move in with other families. But I'm sure that the advantages will progressively seduce a lot of people. It can at least be a solution for young couples who aren't able to find an affordable home in the city, as well as for the elderly who wish to remain self-supporting in a location with lots of social contact.

Move house when you want

The sharing economy can also stimulate residential flexibility. Buying a house and paying loan installments takes so much effort that even thinking about moving is tiring. This is what Isabelle Vermeir, CEO of Century 21 Benelux, has to say:

"Moving closer to work? Living smaller? These are social issues that we hear a lot about. But, in practice it's a distant reality. We're willing to accept being stuck in traffic jams in the morning, in order to keep on living in our own house in a small town."[34] The sharing economy may be a great milestone to exit this deadlock, especially if the trend is moving towards a platform model, like the already existing car sharing platforms. People will stop personally investing in a project, and instead choose a subscription plan allowing them to use housing units and share common space. No longer owners of their own homes, they can be flexible and move to a new type of accommodation that answers their needs at a given time.

Residential flexibility also encourages co-existence in smaller spaces. And it's a necessity. The mobility issues won't find a solution if we keep on going back and forth from the most remote areas. The price paid by society to maintain our current lifestyle is simply too high. Social costs have been supported by the population for years. If the true costs of suburban housing developments were charged to the residents, change would happen very quickly.[35]

Buying a house without a real estate attorney or notary?

Digital technology can modify residency patterns, as well as house buying patterns. Today, everybody needs a notary (or, depending of the country, a "closing notary", "real estate attorney" or "notary signing agent") to register the act of purchase. Even if the buying or selling transaction is fairly simple, fees can rapidly run up. The new "blockchain" technology can significantly reduce these fees. We've already heard about this new technology through its use in virtual currencies, such as the bitcoin, but other practical applications are possible. "You can believe me: this will go beyond the internet," rejoices American web entrepreneur Patrick Byrne.[36] The fact is that blockchain technology can fundamentally modify the way all transactions are carried out. At present, everything is centralized. Let's take the example of a real estate sale: the cadastral surveyor handles all transactions and the notary has an intermediate function. He verifies and registers them in cadasters. Blockchain allows the transaction to happen in a transparent and safe manner, at a lower cost. Basically, blockchain is a public register of all transactions on a network. The transactions aren't registered by a registration entity, but on all computers connected to the network. Transparency is ensured, because all transactions are registered on multiple computers. Also, the chain is extremely secure: in order to defraud or falsify information, you'd have to enter each computer on the network due to the fact that all changes need to be approved on each computer in the chain. And the technology doesn't need the intervention of third parties, because blockchain's network verifies each transaction by itself. In theory, a property sale and the registration of the transaction could be handled bilaterally, by two people, without the need for a notary. Without intermediaries, the blockchain can reduce the costs of real estate transactions. That doesn't mean the end of notaries. "The principal function of a notary is to advise about and take responsibility for a transaction. A computer can't do that. If the blockchain frees us from administrative tasks, more time is left for tasks that require more of an intellectual contribution," explains the Belgian Federation of Notaries.[37] If the registration of the transaction is done with the blockchain technology, the notary can focus on his or her principal tasks: checking if all the certifications are complete, making sure that the seller doesn't have any debts, or ensuring that the property isn't located in a flood zone.

Several interesting start-ups are experimenting with the possibilities of big data in the real estate sector. Realo, for example, wants to improve housing searches by adding criteria such as "located near schools" and "easy access to public transport", but also to automate and make objective assessments of the property based on historical data and the neighborhood's characteristics. It's not difficult to imagine that optimization must be possible, especially when one sees how real estate agents sometimes make rough estimates regarding properties (often with enormous differences).

3D printing a house

Despite technological progress, we continue to build our houses as we've done for hundreds of years. Brick after brick, the mason does his job. One after the other, different building professions succeed each other, sometimes even correcting the errors of their predecessors. In certain cases, a great deal of the construction budget is spent to take down what was just built, to make it right. Let's use the example of the incredible mess at the new Berlin-Brandenburg airport construction site. Work started in 2006. The objective was to open the airport in 2011. Seven years after the deadline, the airport is still not finished and its inauguration in 2019 remains unsure.[38] The reason being a huge list of construction errors: thousands of fire doors that don't close correctly, parking lots that collapsed only weeks after construction, kilometers of wire badly placed and not enough passenger check-in counters.

It's unprecedented and the construction of this airport is an ongoing saga, but on a much smaller scale, this is exactly what happens on other construction sites. No one is going to deny that the construction of a building is complicated. The same applies to a plane. A Boeing 747 is made with over 6 million parts and 250 kilometers of wire. However, jumbo-jets don't crash regularly because of manufacturing defects. Aircraft manufacturers have no margin for error and no one would accept it if they made as many mistakes as many construction companies do. In reality, there's no reason to hold it against the construction sector. All things considered, the sector was weakly consolidated and housing units are mostly built by small companies. By working on a small scale, the construction sector has, in a certain way, forgotten to get on the industrialization train. Profitability and efficiency can be greatly improved.

3D printing is also a technology that holds great promises for the construction sector. On YouTube you can easily find videos of Chinese houses entirely constructed with the help of a 3D printer. During the process, a mixture of cement and construction waste is ejected by an enormous printer, layer after layer until the house is built. This is how a Chinese company succeeded in printing a dozen houses in just 24 hours.[39]

In Shanghai, complete apartment buildings and villas emerge from 3D printers; the technology is also used in the United States and in Russia. The big advantage is that a 3D printer offers amazing precision, to the millimeter: it doesn't build a crooked wall after a night out in the city. This type of printer doesn't build a house in a single operation, but it prints one wall at a time and assembles them. Consequently, they can be built in a sheltered area, protected from rain and wind, as is sometimes done with prefab houses.

© Shutterstock

Print your house in 24 hours for less than 3300 euros with ICON (express.be).

Peter-Paul van den Berg has a positive vision of the future: "3D printers present numerous advantages for the construction sector. It's quicker. (...) Labor costs can be reduced by 50 to 80%. Therefore, the contractor's final invoice is reduced. 60% less waste is produced and recovered waste can be recycled and used as raw materials. So, it is all good for the environment. Also, 3D printers allow more creativity, custom-made work and last-minute changes without extra charges and soaring costs."[40] 3D printing is also a solution to the structural problem of the labor shortage in the construction sector.[41]

A 3D printer offers amazing precision, to the millimeter: it doesn't build a crooked wall after a night out on the town.

Virtual reality technology can make a major contribution to home construction as well. The drawings are often still printed on paper and may sometimes have a few 3D images that are of little use. Virtual reality will bring more life to architects' drawings, and offer them a better vision of their work, while preventing errors that might have been made otherwise. Imagine walking around in your home even before it has been built. A lot of unfortunate surprises could be avoided this way.

Add a touch of artificial intelligence and the computer will be able to accomplish a series of standard tasks such as laying in the water lines and electricity.

Imagine walking around in your home even before it has been built.

And let's not forget drones. Those little remote-controlled aircraft are increasingly being used on construction sites to perform different tasks, such as measuring, inspection and surveillance. Risky activities could be done by drones. United, all these innovations allow a structural decrease of costs and reduce the ecological impact of construction in Digitalis.

Talking houses

Home automation has aroused curiosity for several decades now. In the 1971 French movie *The Burglars* (with Jean-Paul Belmondo and Omar Sharif) there's a famous scene in an apartment where the lights go on and off by hand clapping. The scene is followed by a funny moment when each time Belmondo slaps a playmate the lights go on and off. It's no surprise that fascination with these "technological gadgets" is growing, because at that time numerous new household appliances made their appearance. Think of the washing machines and dishwashers that came into the households in the 70s and 80s. Applications were still limited and technology was very expensive. Also, every electrical appliance had wires that ran over the floor, walls and ceilings. It was complicated to replace a home automation system that became obsolete within only a few years. That's why home automation never really took off. Until now.

Wi-Fi technology has changed everything. It's no longer necessary to have work done to connect all of your devices with wires. All you need is a small device, fixed to the wall, to connect all sorts of devices to the wireless internet. This is why today we can talk about *smart homes* or intelligent houses. Not so long ago, it was unthinkable, but now, even an old house like mine can use home automation. I control the lighting and the heating with my smartphone. Nest, the home automation branch of Alphabet, introduced its first product in 2011: the Nest Learning Thermostat, designed to optimize the heating and cooling of a house in order to save energy. More applications appeared in the following years, such as smoke detectors, surveillance cameras and intelligent alarm systems. Meanwhile, smartphones are no longer the exclusive domain of tech companies. Energy producers Eneco and ENGIE offers the Boxx system. It allows clients to map their energy consumption and easily verify if additional energy savings are possible. The system also knows when to turn up the heat and you can regulate it when you're away from home, for example if you are away longer than expected. Wi-Fi use makes the technology really flexible: people can easily go from one system to another and continuously add new devices. It has lowered the threshold so that today, every house can benefit from one of the kinds of home automation available.

We are only at the beginning of intelligent housing. As always, it starts with appealing gadgets, especially attractive to those who are really fascinated by technology. Being able to control the lighting in my home from my smartphone is not going to change my life radically. However, the thermostat is a different story. By adapting the heating control, the comfort level of my home increases while my electric bill is reduced by 20 to 30%. The thermostat "senses" when someone is at home and adapts the temperature accordingly. It's possible to turn the heating off and on from a distance. Very practical when you're on your way home from a holiday and you want to step into a nice warm house, or when you've forgotten to turn off the heat before leaving the house.

The June energy service is a good example.[42] June places several sensors on your gas and electricity meters in order to monitor your consumption. Based on the findings, you will automatically be switched to another provider so that you can always take advantage of the best prices. Nuki is another interesting example.[43] This company makes intelligent locks. They fit almost any door and offer access to your house from a distance. You can send a temporary key to your housekeeper's smartphone so she can enter your house at a given time. A connected surveillance camera allows you to check if the work is done correctly. Little by little our houses will become completely automated thanks to the virtual assistant. First, it appeared on smartphones and smart speakers, but today it can be found anywhere in your home.[44] Amazon created the virtual assistant Alexa, embedded in the Echo smart speaker. The Google Assistant is incorporated in the Google Home speaker and Apple has launched the HomePod. They started off as "just" voice-activated speakers used to control other devices and today they have evolved into screen applications. In the very near future, televisions will no longer be controlled by remote controls, but will listen to your voice. It is no co-incidence that the electronics company Samsung has developed Bixby, their own virtual assistant already incorporated in their new televisions. Numerous producers cherish higher ambitions than just the simple voice control and don't want to be the under-dogs competing with Google and Amazon. LG, for example, wants to control all its household appliances with their own artificial in-telligence system, called Thinq. The South Korean giant men-tions a few examples of situations where it could be useful, but they are not very convincing. This one for example: you have a chicken in your refrigerator and you are looking for a recipe on the incorporated door screen. As soon as you've picked a recipe, Thinq will switch on the LG oven and set it to the right tempera-ture. It can also pick the appropriate washing program on your

Washing machines, dishwashers and vacuum cleaners were, according to many people, just "gadgets" that would never find their way into every home.

LG dishwasher. Thanks to the new technology, the refrigera-tor sends an order to the su-permarket's online shop to or-der milk, when it notices you are running out. Informed of the dinner details, the system will propose the best food and wine pairing.

All these applications are still in the gadget stage, but this technology is starting to heat up and reach a greater public. The world where voice control screens are naturally incorporated into our homes, in order to make our lives easier, is closer than we think.

The same way washing machines, dishwashers and vacuum cleaners did in the past. Don't forget that, initially, many people considered these appliances just "gadgets" that would never find their way into every home.

Smart
cities

A city can be compared to a gigantic house. Digital technology doesn't only reinvent housing, it also changes the cities we live in. Today, we're talking about smart cities. These are cities where information technology and the internet of things are used for urban management, in terms of administration as well as facilities, such as libraries, hospitals, transport and public services. The aim of these systems is to improve the quality of life and create better city organization to bridge the gap between citizens and administration. Every component in the city is linked through a network of sensors, internet and technological devices.[45]

Let's turn to Singapore for a fine example of a *smart city*. In 2014, the city-state deployed its *Smart Nation* program. The authorities installed an unprecedented number of cameras and sensors, which record and store everything that happens. This is why *smart cities* are so open to criticism: they only function with enormous amounts of collected data, which raises the question of privacy rights (see the chapter *Trust Digitalis*). But all this data is registered and transformed into a myriad of applications for citizens' use. An intelligent city is well aware of available parking spaces and sends a notification to residents and commuters to signal where they can park. Traffic lights are automatically controlled to improve traffic flow or change to green when an ambulance is coming. Museums and cultural centers are connected to a network that tells visitors when is the best time to visit or at what time they can get on the next tramway to get to their destination.

An intelligent city also registers water and energy fluctuations in order to adapt its provision accordingly. It changes the way that cities approach the energy question. Today, the energy production is entirely based on the principles of the industrial era: big energy plants generate as much energy as possible and then redistribute it to everyone. This is an outdated model, as we are moving forward towards to decentralized production. Houses and companies have solar panels on their roofs or wind turbines to produce their own energy. The system is not yet 100% reliable, because it's difficult to manage production and usage peaks and valleys. As there's less sun in winter, there's less solar energy produced, but the electricity needs are higher. Tesla has already developed gigantic lithium-ion batteries capable of storing enough energy to meet the energy needs of 30,000 homes for one hour and in case of a power outage. The Tesla battery recharges with the surplus electricity from a nearby wind energy farm.[46]

All of this shows the importance of the changes happening in Digitalis. The new digital technology modifies our way of building, occupying our homes, and most of all living. This is why the world's appearance will increasingly change as digitalization intensifies.

CHAPTER 5

A self-driving car on demand

How do we reinvent mobility?

Even if I do my best to use public transport as much as I can, I often have to take my car in the morning from the south of Antwerp to get to the center of Brussels. When I first started working for Google, six years ago, I could leave at 6:30 am and arrive at the office only half an hour later, without getting stuck in heavy traffic. Last year, I had to leave at 6:00 am to avoid traffic jams and today I have to leave fifteen minutes earlier. The word *mobility* has lost all meaning. Everybody rants about never-ending traffic jams, which start earlier each time and follow one after ter another. Multiplying or widening expressways is not the solution. What we need to do is reinvent mobility.

The sharing economy generates new forms of mobility making it unnecessary to get around all the time by (personal) car. Moreover, a lot of travelling can be avoided.

Digitalization offers unique opportunities. Self-driving cars are no longer a futurist gadget: the Waymo branch of Alphabet already has 600 cars cruising American roads and, without a doubt, within the coming years we'll see them on our roads in Europe too. Initially, they'll make driving more comfortable by optimizing traffic flow. But that's not their real value: ultimately, self-driving cars will make personally owned cars redundant. This is how a new era is going to arise, where buying a car is no longer necessary. A simple application will allow you to have one at your disposal at all times. The vision we have of mobility will change profoundly, as will the quality of life in our cities and towns.

While waiting for self-driving cars to come our way, digitalization already offers us several solutions. The sharing economy generates new forms of mobility making it unnecessary to get around all the time by (personal) car. Also, a lot of travelling can be avoided thanks to the large range of ways to communicate that are provided by the digital evolution.

Mobility
of the last century

A lot of us will need a mental switch to be able to welcome the principles of the new mobility. That's why it's so important to realize how much current mobility is a product of the past industrial revolution. It's spiritual father? Henri Ford. He introduced assembly line production even before the First World War and, in doing so, he laid the foundations of mass production. Cars literally drove off the assembly lines one after another. Cars have become a part of mass production and accessible to almost everyone.

This evolution can be credited with providing mobility for millions of people who had never really gotten beyond the borders of their own towns. Meanwhile, we have to acknowledge that mobility has exploded beyond our control and a great number of cities have to deal daily with structural traffic jams.

Additionally, we all have to pay the price personally. Traffic jams cause stress and make inefficient use of our time. The American company Inrix deals with traffic information from all around the world in real time and each year publishes the *Traffic Scorecard*. In 2017, it calculated that drivers lost an average of 39 hours in and around Brussels.[47] How many people get to work in the morning in a state of frustration and stress after a drive of 2 hours? When my children were little, I could hardly ever have breakfast with them or take them to school if I wanted to get to work on time. I tried at least to not miss dinner. I wasn't always that lucky. The trip home varied from taking 25 minutes to an hour and a half, sometimes even longer.

What's more, the increase in traffic can prove deadly. On a global scale, automobile accidents result in the deaths of 1.2 million people each year.[48] Add the deaths caused by car pollution and it seems clear that it's urgent to take action.[49] Maybe we have to start by completely rethinking mobility, because all those traffic jams insidiously poison the whole of our society.

On a global scale, automobile accidents result in the deaths of 1.2 million people each year. Add the deaths caused by car pollution and it seems clear that it's urgent to take action.

From ownership
to availability

For a lot of families, a car is the second major purchase, right after a house. However, it's not a good investment. We take it to drive to work, where it sits in a parking lot all day. Then we drive home and park the car in front of our house, while we watch TV and sleep. So, over 95% of the time, the car doesn't move, even if we've easily invested 15,000 euros or more in it. And still, a lot of people really want to own a car. The digital evolution can completely overthrow this trend.

In the previous chapters, I've given a broad outline of how digital society shifts from possession to providing availability. The era of ownership has passed. What about the way we consume music? In the past, we bought a CD that was put away in a cabinet. Today, we subscribe to music streaming services. We no longer physically own the music, but we can listen to it as often as we like and mobile devices make it possible to listen wherever we are. Of course, the difference between not owning any more CDs or DVDs and getting rid of your car is huge. Most people are truly attached to owning a vehicle. It will take time to change mentalities. The car is some sort of social status symbol that we use to display and show who we are. And that might be precisely what's going to trigger the change. In the near future, purchasing a self-driving car will have a symbolic value (as the purchase of a Tesla does today). Then, a growing portion of the population, and even companies linked to mobility, will progressively integrate the concept, until owning a personal car loses its cachet and everyone uses a self-driving car. Self-driving cars will become just simple cars. And as soon as everybody uses a self-driving car, it will be logical to use the car with the perspective of availability instead of possession. Why buy a car if we don't drive it personally?

The sharing economy is already changing mobility. Shared bicycle services have already appeared in a lot of cities. Users check out a bicycle from one station and check it back in in another station. There's nothing better if you want to travel small distances in a city.

Free-floating bike sharing (bicycles you can leave anywhere in the city once you've rented them) has met with great success in several cities. The success of these services is proof that urban and communal entities should invest a lot more. It's very profitable, as demonstrated by Denmark. Policies regarding cyclists have made Copenhagen the European cycling capital. Approximately 62% of the residents get on their bikes to go to school or to work[50], which is remarkable for a city where the temperature is a lot lower and where it snows more often than in a lot of cities that are further south.

Platforms, such as Drive Now, also encourage car sharing. In the past, you had to go to a rental agency to arrange for a car. A contract of several pages needed to be read and signed and you couldn't rent a car for less than a day. It was complicated, expensive and not very flexible. Someone without a car would have never thought of going to a rental agency just to get a car to do the grocery shopping. But with car sharing platforms it's now possible. Younger people don't have to own a car, but can use these platforms to rent one, based on their needs. For a few hours or a couple of days. Users book a car on a mobile application, pick up the car at one of the gathering points and pay afterwards, in proportion to their actual usage.

A European version of the Uber App?

The pinnacle of car sharing is Uber of course. This American web company has, in particular, developed an application that allows travelers and private drivers to get in contact with each other in over 600 cities around the world. This car sharing system is a good alternative solution to taxis and public transport, as it's often less expensive and much faster. Taxis are relatively expensive relative to the friendliness and the quality of service provided. We aren't always sure if the taxi driver knows how to get to the requested address and it's not good for the client when the driver pretends that the electronic payment device is out of order or when he says he has no change when you pay cash. This causes frustration for the passenger, as well as for other drivers, when the taxi is not moving while you're trying to pay for the trip.

The Uber application resolves all these problems. All you need to do is to register and follow the arrival of the Uber car on your smartphone. The driver knows exactly where you are thanks to the same application. Payments are done automatically and the rates are transparent. This transparency and simplicity have allowed Uber to progress worldwide at a rapid pace: from students who use it to go home after a night out, to businesspeople who go from meeting to meeting when they are on business in town. A lot of Parisians no longer purchase a car, because parking spaces are too expensive in the city. They prefer getting around with Uber. A sharing platform like this one, allows for trips to be optimized, as they are transparent, cheap and user-friendly. It is indeed possible to reach the city with public transport, to avoid traffic jams, and use the sharing platform to go from one meeting to another.

This potential is not limited to the city alone. Sharing plat-forms can also be a solution for mobility issues in rural areas. It's very difficult to offer a vast range of public transport at a rea-sonable price and therefore it's necessary to develop new ways of mobility. Imagine that you live in a village in the south of France, just a few kilometers from Lyon, and you'd like to go out in the city on a Saturday night. Getting there by public transport might be possible. But after 10:00 pm, there's no way to get back home. The only alternative solutions would be to hire a taxi (if they're available, and it would be very expensive) or ride a bike (if you're in good physical condition).

In a way, a car-sharing platform is like individualized public transport. There are enough car owners who don't drink alcohol and would be happy to earn a few euros to bring the kids home safely. This could even be some sort of social commitment, be-cause these types of initiatives can encourage young people to continue living in small towns while keeping the roads safe.

Even if traditional taxi services were afraid for their jobs when Uber came around, they haven't disappeared at all. The two systems coexist side by side in numerous cities and, most-ly, we are witnessing a growth in demand. It's unfortunate that the authorities in European countries have reacted with such tension about the arrival of Uber, or have even completely for-bidden it. They are passing up an opportunity. And that's not only valid for Uber. The fact is that sharing platforms can use fundamental improvements. I'm not just talking about the fu-ture, but about the present. Instead of condemning innova-tion, we need to welcome it. It's up to the authorities to stimu-late it. For starters, they need to suspend the strict rules and regulations that govern the traditional taxi sector, because it has allowed taxis to gain an untouchable monopoly. Other ac-tors have been kept out of the market and the sector has not felt the necessity to innovate, which could be an explanation for the poor service often received. At the same time, it's important that the competition between classic taxi services and sharing platforms remains healthy. The strong fiscal pressure that affects the traditional sector needs to be reduced and digital companies need to be put in a fiscal framework. In that respect, the Belgian authorities have already made a step in the right direction. Since last year, it is possible to earn up to 6000 euros a year of tax-free extra income through recognized sharing platforms. Anyone who earns more has to pay taxes on all earnings.[51] Such initiatives may bring some fresh air into our own European platforms.

We now need to find alternative European solutions to the American application Uber. It's necessary to understand things correctly. Not the way it was done by an Antwerp taxi company. They clearly wanted to respond to the appearance of sharing platforms by creating their own application. It seemed like a good idea to me: I downloaded the application and ordered a taxi straight away. But it never came. When I called the taxi company, I was told that there was no guarantee that a taxi ordered through the application would really show up. The application had not sent me any notifications. This shows that the taxi company has absolutely not understood Uber's message. It's not so much about the App as it is about customer service. The client wants to receive a cheap, efficient and user-friendly service; and they want it quickly. That's possible. For example, take a look at the application German App MyTaxi that is very successful in Dublin.

Self-driving cars
versus phantom traffic jams

The combination of sharing platforms and self-driving cars is really going to revolutionize mobility. Why buy a car when a simple application allows you to use a self-driving car when you really need it? It will drive you to work while you're reading the newspaper, drop you off and then it will go get another passenger. The car will only be used to move around; parking spaces in the city won't be useful anymore, because the self-driving cars will drive from one passenger to another, before going to the outskirts of the city to recharge their batteries. The face of the world will change completely. Parking space issues will be solved and cities will no longer be disfigured by huge parking lots. Pedestrians and cyclists will be able to benefit from public spaces in complete safety. Cities will be given back to their citizens, instead of the car-king.

Thanks to self-driving cars, mobility can be adapted to the needs of each trajectory. A small car is more than efficient to drive someone to work; whilst for a family holiday a bigger car can be used. In addition to more comfort, it's important to mention the effect on the environment. Not only are self-driving cars more efficient and therefore less polluting, but traffic jams full of big (polluting) cars, which often only transport one person, will also disappear thanks to this new mobility. However, some studies claim that self-driving cars will cause more traffic jams. Firstly, researchers think that more people, including kids and the elderly, will use self-driving cars to get around. Also, they're afraid that companies will feel less concerned by the excess of cars, because it allows for work to be done on the road and less time will be lost. It's true, but they underestimate the beneficial effects on traffic fluidity. It's simply difficult to imagine the degree to which self-driving cars can improve traffic and the solutions they can offer: for example, improved organization of carpooling or a proliferation of small cars.

Before getting to the stage where it's possible to use a self-sufficient transport service, it's likely that people will start by buying their own self-driving cars. There will be advantages, because the self-driving car is less dangerous and moves better in traffic. There are plenty videos on YouTube on *phantom traffic jams*. It concerns the strange, sudden, slowing of traffic for no specific reason (accident or road construction), and that resolves itself in the same miraculous way. "Where does this traffic jam come from," we ask ourselves. The reason is that we are all very bad drivers. The roads are so heavily crowded that the margin for error is quite small. Yet, that's what people do: make mistakes. All it takes for a driver is to follow the car in front too closely and all of a sudden hit the brakes, for the next driver to brake harder and the next one harder still and so on. Hundreds of cars further down, everybody has come to a stop and a traffic jam has been created. This phenomenon has been recorded by researchers from the University of Illinois. They conducted an experiment where twenty cars went around in circles, within a big circle. Without any obstacles, the cars drive perfectly fine, until one of them brakes and then continues on its way. In no time, a ripple effect occurred and all of the cars came to a stop. Then, the researchers tell all of the drivers to start and drive in circles again. Only this time a self-driving car has been added to the circle. That was all it took for the circle to keep turning without interruption. Human drivers continued playing with the brakes, but the self-driving car kept its optimal stopping distance and only used the brakes when necessary. Consequently, the other cars slowed down less and the number of braking maneuvers was considerably lowered. Now, imagine what would happen if 10% of the cars on the highway were self-driving. This is not a futurist prediction. "The level of autonomy required to have this effect isn't the kind that Waymo, Uber, and others are seeking to build—it's more akin to the adaptive cruise control already featured in many higher-end cars. So while we might have to wait a little longer for all of autonomy's effects to be felt, its ability to reduce traffic congestion could be here rather sooner than we anticipated," concludes the tech magazine *MIT Technology Review*.[52]

Also, cars controlled by computers are safer in such a way that self-driving cars could potentially reduce the number of road deaths. Worldwide, human errors are responsible for approximately 94% of deadly accidents.[53] In this context, machines and computers are more reliable: they don't drink, they're never distracted and never tired. Twenty years or so from now, it will be hard to believe that humans were in charge of driving big ten-ton trucks.

The self-driving car will get here faster than imagined

Self-driving cars are still in the development phase, but they no longer belong to the distant future. When I would speak about this five years ago, everybody treated me as if I were crazy. Today, 600 Waymo cars cruise the American roads. They have already travelled 12 million kilometers in completely autonomous mode, after having driven 1.6 billion in a simulator in 2016.[54] Uber and several Chinese companies are also on it. Sure, we are still far from achieving widespread use of the self-driving car, but the way I see it, it's not thirty years that we have to wait, but more likely only five to ten. Companies that have already

One of Waymo's self-driving minivans

invested massively in the development of self-driving cars are doing everything they can to secure a fast return on their investment.

Now that we've started to realize that the self-driving car is no illusion, disbelief is being replaced by fear. Any incident implicating a self-driving car will be commented on by every media outlet worldwide, even if serious accidents are extremely rare. Most of the accidents are also caused by humans. For example, when others drivers hit a self-driving car. The fact remains that nightmare scenarios exist. "Self-driving cars programmed to decide who dies in a crash." This was a recent headline[55] that made it around the world. The author of this article was wondering how a self-driving car would react if a bus appeared out of nowhere in front of the car so that it would be impossible to prevent an accident.

Would the car change its course and risk the lives of its passengers? Would it carry out a dangerous avoidance maneuver that would send the bus full of children into a tree? Or would it hit the bus full-on risking the lives of its passengers and those on the bus? It's completely absurd to imagine a scenario like this one, as self-driving cars offer a maximum degree of safety, which is

Companies that have already invested massively in the development of self-driving cars are doing everything they can to secure a fast return on their investment.

proven by the millions of kilometers they have already driven. Besides, avoiding all accidents is impossible. We are never protected from the unexpected: a falling tree, an animal or child running in front of the car... But, a human driver can't do anything about this either. Moreover, even with this type of accident, the self-driving car will always have a better reaction, it being faster-thinking and more alert. The number of road deaths can only be reduced.

This actually says more about the fear and the mistrust each new technological breakthrough brings with it. We can easily make the comparison with the way the whole world burst out laughing when Elon Musk made the announcement in 2004 that Tesla was starting the production and commercial distribution of electrical cars on a large scale. A few years later, when it was clear that the electrical car would make its appearance on the market, the media did their utmost to prove that this new technology was very limited. And yet, Tesla cars are now on the road and some models can even move through traffic autonomously. In 2016, the producer of electrical cars had supplied 76,230 cars to clients, and more than 100,000 in 2017.

By 2020, Tesla wants to sell 1 million cars a year.[56] This is how Tesla created a shock wave that changed the whole of the automo-

A new technology is often considered ridiculous at first, then dangerous, and finally as a solution that's obvious to everyone.

bile sector. Traditional automakers now also offer electric or hybrid cars. A new technology is often considered ridiculous at first, then dangerous, and finally as a solution that's obvious to everyone.

Are truck drivers doomed to unemployment?

Have you always dreamt of a self-driving car? Truck drivers probably haven't, because self-driving trucks are also in the making. In 2016, ABInBev caused quite a stir in the American state of Colorado when a commercial delivery was made by a self-driving truck. The Belgian beer giant's heavy truck really did transport a load of Budweiser over 190 kilometers. A driver was on board, but he could comfortably read a book. Experiments are also being pursued in Europe, especially on big company sites. The self-driving trucks obviously don't need a driver anymore. This is where the horrible nightmare of thousands of jobs lost because of the new technology pops up. What is really going on?

First of all, self-driving cars and trucks aren't for today. Their arrival will surely take place within five or ten years from now and total replacement of the entire fleet will take another several years. This leaves enough time for the job market to get ready. What's more, a career as a truck driver doesn't attract a lot of people anymore. Bus and truck driver jobs are on top of the sensitive jobs list, meaning that employers have a hard time finding good candidates. Driving in bumper-to-bumper traffic day in and day out, working under high pressure and with irregular hours…we can't say that these are working conditions you'd want to write home about.

It's not because certain jobs are disappearing that other jobs won't exist. Whatever the ingenuity of the technology used for a self-driving truck, it still remains a vehicle with wheels and mechanical and electronic components. There will always be a need for mechanics, maybe even more so than today. "It's true that we won't be seeing thousands of truck drivers on our roads in the coming years. In the meantime, some of them will have received training to become mechanics. This retraining shouldn't take any longer than three months, because who knows the trucks better than those who drive them thousands of kilometers a year?" declared Jacques van den Broek, CEO of the recruiting company Randstad, during a congress in Amsterdam about the future of employment. That being said, not all truck drivers will be mechanics. But digitalization also creates other jobs and requires new skills. I am convinced that everyone can access a good profession by receiving good retraining. Even better: today's truck drivers will have more comfortable, safer and healthier jobs. Besides, some truck drivers still will be needed to supervise the journey as well as the loading and unloading.

The joys of telecommuting

Digitalization doesn't only make it easier to move around. It also allows you to spend less time on the road while working from home. All smartphones, tablets and laptops support video-conferencing without the need for special software programs or expensive stand-alone devices. An internet connection and a mobile device are all it takes to organize a meeting with colleagues who are in Lisbon or Shanghai for example. Thus, it is no longer necessary for you to be at the office all the time. Yet, telecommuting is not anchored in professional practices. For example, only 8% of Belgians make use of telecommuting. They work an average of one day per week from home or in a satellite office close to their home, resulting in a 2% reduction in traffic. This means that there are lower CO_2 emissions and less air pollution. More important maybe: if we could double the number of telecommuters, in Belgium 25 fewer people would die or get badly hurt in road accidents every year.[57] However, the concept often meets with a lot of resistance because we are still steeped in the principles that were hammered into us by the previous industrial revolutions.

Control and performance, those were the key words in the industrial era. Each worker had to be present at 9:00 am and the boss used a time clock to verify each and every worker's presence. At 5:00 pm, everyone could go home. Not a minute earlier. The time clock has disappeared from many workplaces, but it continues to function in our heads. Too many managers still believe that their employees should come to the office, how else can management keep an eye on them? It's about time to bury this vision of management. Managers need to let go and trust their employees. At Google, everyone benefits from a great deal of autonomy. We put a lot of time into recruiting, because we want to be sure of the motivation of our new colleagues and be assured that they have totally understood the mission that will be theirs. This kind of colleague often knows better than the manager how to succeed. Make no mistake about it: the employees know how to divide their time between moments they really need to be at the office and when they can work from home.

Does this mean that there are never any problems? No, of course not! Everybody has the same autonomy, without it being constantly controlled. But those who make excessive use of it, are inexperienced, or those who don't do their jobs the way they should be done, will be invited to talk about it and get some help. As a manager, this is a big change for me. Instead of spending my time organizing and supervising my team, it only happens occasionally that I have to help a difficult case back on track. The time that's freed up translates into increased productivity and a more rewarding job for the employee.

All managers should try telecommuting at their companies. How? First, you need to understand why it can be useful. Then you get on with it. All that is needed now, is to observe the positive effects and the way employees grow. When relevant, sometimes it's necessary to correct errors and inefficiencies. It's obvious that telecommuting is not for everyone. A technician who handles a machine has to be present at the job site. The same goes for a receptionist who needs to welcome guests and visitors. But today's rule that requires almost every employee to be present at the workplace should become an exception. A small number of workers will always have to be present at the workplace because of the nature of their jobs, but for most of them, flexibility is called for.

No telecommuting without new technology

It will take more than a mindset shift for managers to make telecommuting the new norm. We're living in the 21st century and we all own a masterpiece of technology, a tablet or a smartphone. But sometimes time seemed to have stopped ticking at the workplace. Some employees still have to work on old computers like the AS400 (a series launched by IBM in 1988), using operating systems like Windows98, Lotus Notes or other prehistoric fossils. There is nothing as easy as calling your child, who's on holiday in Australia, via Skype; but when a videoconference needs to be organized with another division of the company, you have to start by contacting the IT manager. Telecommuting can only be efficient when colleagues can share their calendars, plan meetings with the help of automatic notifications, and be able to easily organize a videoconference. A lot of companies overestimate the costs the investments this may require. In the past, we were talking about a series of major costs. When I was still working for the media group Corelio/Mediahuis, we invested 30,000 euros in 2011 in an application that allowed videoconferences between the head office in Brussels and our Namur branch *L'Avenir*. A video system had to be installed at both locations in a space that turned out to be too small to hold the entire executive team. The technology worked fine, but the user-friendliness and the price were not in balance.

Today, a lot of affordable applications exist. They allow employees to get started for only a few dozen euros a year. The technology is often less expensive than it used to be, thanks to the evolution of cloud computing and software as a service. Companies no longer have to invest in expensive services, because they rent the necessary storage capability in the cloud. And they don't need to spend a lot of money on software programs either, considering that they can also be used on a subscription basis. Investment costs disappear to make way for operating costs. This is a more flexible solution that doesn't eat up a big part of the companies' capital. A good example is gSuite, Google's company package. Employees can use it to send emails, save files and deal with documents. Google Hangouts allows them to participate in videoconferences. All of this is available for just 40 euros per user per year. In other words, a team of ten managers can have access to all tools they need for telecommuting for a global cost of 400 euros per year. Now, compare that to the 30,000 euros from my previous job...

Many companies don't grasp the speed with which the world is evolving and stubbornly hang on to their own IT systems. Not only does it cost them a lot of money, but it also takes a toll on their productivity.

I've estimated that Hangouts and gSuite help me save easily 30% of my time, because I travel less, my meetings don't last as long, and I optimize my participation. A member of my executive team even takes part in meetings when he's away. He parks his car, participates in the videoconference and then gets back on the road again.

The question of the company car

As frustrating as it is, we all got used to traffic. But if the people from the 1960s were to travel forward in time and experience today's road fever, we would be witnesses of an instant popular uprising. No politician would survive the elections.

Unfortunately, not much is being done to fight traffic congestion in Europe. On the contrary, the company car system that's being used in many countries goes so far as to subsidize those who get stuck behind their steering wheels in traffic. That is beyond comprehension. If we want to resolve the mobility issue, we need to start a fiscal reform that taxes the salaried workforce less in order to eliminate the company car system. Skeptics will claim that traffic jams won't disappear, but people will simply take their own car to get to work. They are partly right: the car is still a popular means of transport; but people behave differently when it's their own car they're driving.

At Google, no one has a company car. Not even the bosses. When I first started my career, I was a bit skeptical myself about this approach. It seemed to me that it was a good deal, especially for the company, because I thought they could boast about reduced CO_2 emissions, when in reality the problem was just shifted to its employees. Nothing was further from the truth. This courageous approach definitely has an immediate effect how much cars are used and consequently pollution. Personally, I exchanged my big SUV for a cute little Mini, which consumes approximately half the fuel. There are no big expensive cars in the parking lot of the Google head office in Belgium, only small, city cars. Also, there are only five parking spaces for the sixty-some employees of the company in Brussels (and no, I don't have my own reserved parking space). It encourages our employees to leave their cars at home and use public transport, which happens more and more as they have to pay for their own cars. And so, they just don't purchase a car, because their partner already has one or simply because it's easy to get to the office with public transport.

Personally, I'd like to take another step and replace my Mini with an electric car. This is completely feasible as our parking has a charging station. All I'd need is a charging station near my home, as I don't have a garage at my house. My city places charging stations on demand, but only after you've already purchased an electric car. The city doesn't guarantee, however, if and when the stations will be placed. I can't buy an electric car, because I don't have charging station and I can't ask for a charging station, because I don't have an electric car. There's a fundamental error in there, somewhere. And really, I wouldn't hesitate to purchase an electric car, if there was a charging station in my area, because today we can find great models. This is a good example of how the authorities could influence our car buying behavior with only a few measures.

Digitalization allows us to completely reinvent mobility in Digitalis. It can't resolve all of our problems by itself in the short term, but it offers real and interesting solutions that could be implemented quickly.

CHAPTER 6

The pleasure of learning

How do we reinvent education?

Our schools are like a rich buffet: they offer a wide choice of subjects to try out. But even if our children aren't hungry, they're forced to eat everything. As delicious as caviar and oysters are, you still need to have an appetite for them. The same goes for education programs. Someone who has no taste for mathematics nevertheless receives an ample portion to sink his teeth into and someone who has no appetite for history must, despite everything, swallow a good-sized serving of it. Passion and enthusiasm can't be imposed by force. It's imperative that we abandon the idea that children won't be able to succeed without suffering. It's a lot more important to identify their talents in order to stimulate these as much as we can. This is the only way to prepare our children for tomorrow's digital society.

No sector of society is as crucial as education. Without education, it would have been impossible for us to move from an agrarian to an industrial society as we did during previous industrial revolutions. Broad segments of the population have been granted access to education or have been given the opportunity to re-educate themselves. From generation to generation, it's been possible to work at safer, healthier jobs. With each new generation, employment has become more stimulating and better paid. This evolution is the basis of our current prosperity and is one of Europe's major assets.

Society today is undergoing a transformation at least as significant as the one that occurred during the industrial revolution. Education is again called upon to play a fundamental role. Everything is changing at an accelerated pace because of the digital evolution. What one learns one day is, as it were, already outdated the day after tomorrow. Children, young people, and adults must learn to deal with permanent change, an overabundance of information, and a multitude of technologies. The digital evolution is leading to radical changes in the job market, requiring new skills, new talents, and functions that did not even exist until recently. Teachers face a dual challenge: preparing children and young people for a new world and retraining adults to make sure they don't miss the digital boat. The world of education will have to reinvent itself in Digitalis.

Learning to cross the digital highway

Starting from primary school, children learn to cross the street properly because traffic is dangerous and it's important to be able to travel safely. In the meantime, a digital highway has been built, but almost no one is giving children and young people a hand in telling them how to approach it. Current education in a lot of European countries doesn't pay much attention to the good aspects of the digital world, nor does it shed light on its potential dangers. And then we're surprised that accidents happen ...

While it's important to teach children how to deal with new digital technologies, it's also important to explain how these technologies work. In order to do this, we have to start teaching them programming as early as possible. Not because we need to make all of them good programmers, but rather to teach them a skill as important as learning to write or crossing the street safely. Computers are part of everyday life and children need to know how to use them. Better yet: being able to program helps one better understand how the world works.

To familiarize children with digital technology, it's obvious that one shouldn't swamp them with boring lessons on theory, but get them interested in a playful way instead. Today, it's easy to teach children how to program small toy robots to perform a series of fun tasks is easy.

Starting from primary school, children learn to cross the street properly because traffic is dangerous and it's important to be able to travel safely. In the meantime, a digital highway has been built, but almost no one is giving children and young people a hand in telling them how to approach it.

In this context, CoderDojo is a great initiative. It's an international non-profit organization that was started in Ireland, which teaches programming to girls and boys aged 7 to 18. Young people are taught a computer language free of charge by volunteers. Given this initiative's success, one may wonder why the education system doesn't include similar initiatives in its programs for all children. There's no reason for programming lessons to be reserved for children whose parents understand the importance of computers. Isn't the mission of teaching to offer the same opportunities to all children?

Familiarizing young people with technology will only work if more attention is given to STEM subjects. STEM stands for

Science, *Technology*, *Engineering* and *Mathematics*. The digital revolution is making the world revolve around technology and electronics. This revolution will only intensify, thereby increasing the demand for citizens with a scientific profile.

The business world is hungry for more technically talented people. For several years, the technical trades have been at the top of the list of professions with a chronic vacancy problem. Many specialist IT positions also remain vacant. This is a problem for an economy running on a technological engine. And above all, a greater diversity in the workplace would also translate to better performing companies and better products; so it's necessary to make a special effort to stimulate girls' enthusiasm for this area.

The school has a leading role to play in the development of new skills spawned by the digital transition. But the practical reality is that there is still much work to do in schools to improve computing resources and teacher training so that they can become effective teaching engines for the future.

Learn
to be an entrepreneur

Focusing on science and technology is not the only aspect of education that needs change. Many university students never have the opportunity to take a management course; these are normally reserved for economics students and future business engineers. It's absurd. All university students should have a management course in the first year of their higher education. Aren't doctors and lawyers entrepreneurs in their own practices? Why should they learn everything by trial and error, while economics graduates receive a solid grounding in management? Even for students who don't finish their degree programs, exposure to entrepreneurship can bear fruit. Who knows: in spite of a disappointing stint at college, someone might have the germ of an idea for an app that will seduce the world. Many entrepreneurs have achieved success and celebrity without completing their studies. Bill Gates, Steve Jobs and Mark Zuckerberg ... all interrupted their university studies prematurely to devote themselves entirely to their businesses.

Our students also have much to learn about presentation techniques. The Americans are very good at this, because conducting presentations and public debates is learned at an early age, and it's part of their basic knowledge. Which is far from the case in all of Europe, yet everything revolves around communication. You must at least be able to sell yourself, for example, when applying for a job. Every hiring manager has often been confronted with candidates desperately trying to express themselves, who are at a loss for words.

This is highly problematic at a time when only a very restricted number of employees are not required to have communication skills. At any rate, it's a basic requirement for young entrepreneurs. Any start-up that wants to make money must be able to describe and promote its idea and business model: to explain everything concisely, with a lot of enthusiasm and even a touch of audacity in order to inspire confidence and convince potential investors. This is the strong point of the Americans. Their ideas are not necessarily better, but they often know how to sell them better than anybody else. This is also true of the English and the Dutch. Why isn't this the case in other countries?

Teaching methods in the digital world

Digitalis must not only reinvent school programs, but also the way new subjects are taught. Video can play a very big role here, because it's the new medium *par excellence* in the digital evolution. It offers unique opportunities to faculty because every teacher doesn't always succeed in presenting difficult subjects, in spite of clear explanations. On YouTube you can find a massive number of videos that dissect, in accessible and entertaining ways, topics as complex as Einstein's theory of relativity or artificial intelligence. It would be a shame not to use them.

Young people have already seized on this new medium. When they do their homework and stumble on a math formula, they search for it on YouTube and quickly find the answer to their question. According to Hal Varian, Google's chief economist, YouTube tutorials are viewed more than 500 million times a day. We currently let young people find these videos by themselves after school hours. This ignores the fact that the school and teachers have an important guiding role to play. By integrating these videos into class hours, not only is knowledge shared in an engaging way, but it also helps students who don't have internet access at home or those who were never encouraged to browse on a video platform in search of interesting educational material.

Video also presents another advantage: students may pause or replay it to deepen their understanding or review difficult passages. This way, everyone can learn the subject at his or her own pace. Some will proceed faster than others, but there is a good chance that all students will understand the material better after watching the relevant video. So even if videos don't yet give fully personalized explanations, it's a first step towards individualized education.

The teaching staff, industrial method

Games are another great form of learning. It's no coincidence that Google employees are often avid gamers. Gaming has helped them acquire very specific skills: they developed refined motor skills, they have learned to resolve a problem while playing, and they have learned to collaborate. For a long time gamers have played not only against a computer, but also on large platforms, with or against other gamers. This is how they learn to collaborate in a large international community. All the skills acquired through this approach fit nicely with the digital economy. Furthermore, gamers are used to getting continuous feedback, because during a game, each action instantly triggers a response. They learn more quickly from their mistakes. In traditional teaching, feedback on exercises, quizzes, or exams is often delayed.

Recognizing that educational games can make a major contribution to teaching, game developers are offering an increasing number of this type of game. While playing, children can explore the world of science through all kinds of experiences involving home, garden, and cooking implements.[58] Schools and teachers are ready to welcome digital learning methods, even if we are still far from using them structurally. In any case, we should let our educational system favor an open culture with feedback. This would speed up students' learning and reinforce their involvement.

The teacher becomes a coach

Let's make one thing clear: the new digital learning methods don't make teachers unnecessary. On the contrary. Above all these learning methods are powerful tools that allow faculty to play a different role. The time when professors/experts passed on their knowledge to a class by giving exactly the same exercises to all the students and expecting the same response from of each of them at year's end, is over. This approach only made sense at a time when the whole population still had to learn to read and write. It was the ideal way to provide a basic education to millions of people in a relatively short period of time. And that has borne fruit, because illiteracy has virtually disappeared from first world countries. But, in the meantime, this method of teaching has become outdated and certainly can't survive in the digital age.

Both games and videos allow young people to process information at their own pace, profoundly transforming the function of the teacher. Instead of lecturing on theory, teachers can now let their students work independently. The same goes for higher education. This is what the university of Brussels, VUB sociologist Ignace Glorieux says: "The way we teach today is not adapted to our time. We are there for two or three hours in front of thousands of students, making more or less captivating remarks. In the meantime, the internet broadcasts splendid videos on topics sometimes as boring as statistical regression. Instead, the teacher should become a moderator who teaches his or her students to collect all the information around them and to bring it all together into a coherent piece that can be discussed or published. We need guest professors who orchestrate active and participatory small group discussions to motivate students. The work resources of the future are already available: the internet, tablets, and YouTube."[59]

Digitalization therefore opens up prospects for transforming the professor/experts who previously just transmitted their knowledge, into motivating coaches who instill the desire to learn and expose hidden talents. In this way young people can discover what they love to do and what subjects they excel in.

"If you judge a fish by its ability to climb a tree, it will live its whole life believing that it's stupid."

This is far from what the educational system practiced during the industrial era, when a student that was highly talented in math could end up repeating a year of school or was sent off in a different direction because of a weakness in language. As Albert Einstein is reported to have said: Everyone is a genius. But if you judge a fish by its ability to climb a tree, it will live its whole life believing that it's stupid. Yet this is precisely what education does all too often, partly because of the way it's set up. School establishments must be transformed into talent platforms that help youth identify their talents in order to exploit these fully in the future. Young people will go much further if given the chance to specialize in what they do best, while settling for the minimum in other basic skills. They will walk to school with a spring in their step and give the best of themselves every day. That's what the business world—and society—needs. We don't need young people who all have the same average level of knowledge, we're looking for passionate people with specific talents—in combination, of course, with minimal mastery of a number of basic skills. For example, it's essential to learn English, especially if you want to work in an international company or do scientific research. This doesn't necessarily mean that you have to know all about Shakespeare.

Unfortunately, this teaching concept still encounters too much resistance. Even if we may hope that the trend is gradually reversing itself, progress is far too slow. Many people still think that young people need to get good grades in every subject. And if they don't, it's often attributed to laziness. This is rooted in our vision of success: we can only succeed in life if we work hard in school and if we are ready to suffer. As if an educational path painstakingly pursued always helped to achieve success; but education keeps trying to drive fish up trees. The critics consider an educational approach that focuses on talent as being too lenient, but that's not the case. If a student were gifted in mathematics, it would be necessary to raise the bar for him or her in this subject. And the ones with a talent for languages, such as English, should set their sights much higher than standard English, and plunge into Shakespeare. Personalized teaching is the key. Technology gives us the tools, but that won't work without inspired teachers acting as coaches. The teaching profession therefore needs to be reassessed, to undergo a renewed appreciation. About fifty years ago the schoolteacher was one of the important people in a town, having the same status as the doctor or the priest. It's no longer like that today—which is a mistake, because teachers have a major influence on the future lives of young people. Many do it out of passion, in spite of the increase in administrative harassment, the loss of motivation in young people, and occasional meddling by parents. It's in our interest to have the most talented people chose a teaching career while ensuring that they can exercise their profession under the best conditions for their role as coaches.

The LAB school in Sint-Amands in the province of Antwerp proves that it's possible. This secondary school opened in September of 2017. It was founded by a few parents and educational experts who wanted to offer an alternative solution to the current school system. Theoretical, personal, and empirical knowledge are used to achieve the objectives set by the LAB school. Although it's not supported by any network, it's recognized and subsidized by the government. Like other recognized schools, LAB must adhere to educational objectives and other foundations of competence. That's why it adheres to a whole set of different principles. "Technological evolution is constantly advancing and there is more and more knowledge. It has become impossible today to stop learning after leaving school. It's therefore better to have a secondary education that makes you want to learn and continue to train: a school where we know why we learn something, or we discover who we are, or we learn to manage setbacks and frustrations, and where we can summon motivation. An enthusiastic teaching body—they are also teachers who choose to step off the beaten path in order to make their students discover this yearning," this is the school's mission.[60]

If teachers are present full-time throughout the week, they won't be standing in front of a single class. In fact, the school has opted for co-teaching alongside independent learning and abandoned the 50-minute lesson plan where each subject is discussed separately. "This type of learning allows you to build bridges. We connect subjects to each other: a language course is ideal for teaching grammar while dealing with a scientific text. This will kill two birds with one stone and will free up time for other things. We wish to devote this time to activities such as art and creation, sport, or research projects. It's also possible to devote effective attention to STEM," explains Kristien Bruggeman, educational scientist and co-director of the new school. When will these fantastic initiatives become widespread?

The digital university

Not only does digitalization change the content and methods of teaching, but it also guarantees access to education. The non-profit organization Take Off has the objective of keeping sick students connected to their class thanks to computers. In one click, children can be put in contact with their class. This non-profit organization was created in 2006 by a trio of volunteers, previous IBM employees. Today, the team consists of a dozen people, volunteers and professionals, of all skill-levels and all ages. From 2006 to 2015, more than 400 children, 14 hospitals, and 230 schools have benefited from Take Off.

Internet teaching has also found a place in universities with the help of MOOC or Massive Open Online Courses. These are online courses open to students around the world. In addition to traditional didactic materials such as conference videos, they provide interactive forums where students, faculty, and assistants can start discussions. The first MOOCs appeared in 2006, but their real breakthrough dates from 2011, when the prestigious American Stanford University organized a MOOC on artificial intelligence. In the context of a classically organized course, there would have been no more than a few dozen students present in the audience, but thanks to the MOOC, more than 160,000 people had registered. Shortly after, the university announced two other MOOCs that each time reached the milestone of 100,000 registrations. It was large-scale education, the like of which had never been seen before. The university was initially very reluctant to help make a course accessible to the whole world. Why should it offer this for free, when other students pay tens of thousands of dollars to register at the University? But thanks to the perseverance of the project initiators, Stanford professors have finally reached a global audience, thus providing valuable advertising for the university. Stanford University has not lost a single student and has found a whole new audience. This perfectly illustrates that universities will not disappear because of the digital revolution, but are instead being called upon to fulfill a much broader role than just the transmission of knowledge. "In the near future, it will be possible to provide courses and to learn in any place and at any time. The campus will not be less important. We are immersed in a certain culture. Just for that, this physical place will continue to count," says VUB Professor of Educational Science Chang Zhu.[61]

Continuing education

It's illusory to think that one will never have to study again after having completed one's education. Continuing education until you retire is the new standard in the digital world. Formerly, when people completed their studies, they received a beautiful diploma stamped with a solemn seal upon which their entire career would be built. "It will not work anymore like that for your kids. In a constantly changing world, things work otherwise. The cycle will become shorter and shorter: no career can last longer than thirty years. That's why our teaching must be oriented towards ongoing training. You have to learn to retrain permanently. The taxi driver who would lose his job because of the Uber app must realize that it's still perfectly possible for him to get a degree at a major American university," says Rob Nail, CEO of Singularity University, which is, so to speak, Silicon Valley's educational institution.[62] In the future, we will simply continue to be members of an institution which will continuously train us. Better yet, many specialists will lose their license if they don't continue to retrain regularly. Universities and high schools are evolving into continuing education centers that distribute certificates rather than diplomas.

This means that a lot of responsibility will now rest on each of us individually. It's very easy to lay the blame for getting fired on the digital evolution, and then complain about not being suited for another job. This type of mentality makes a worker a pawn in the reorganization game. You have to personally take charge of your future. The typical counter-argument is that not everybody has sufficient abilities to work at a digital profession and that retraining isn't always possible. The problem here is that retraining elicits a lot of fear. There is no reason for people who have worked all their lives for a car manufacturer to remain in the automotive industry forever. Retraining doesn't necessarily involve reorientation to another function within the same sector. Why shouldn't a metal worker with a green thumb be retrained to work in gardening? Why shouldn't an office worker who got tired of his job become a carpenter? Or why shouldn't a manager turn to teaching? Continuing education can, above all, provide an ideal opportunity to move towards a more digitally-oriented career. Lifelong learning and retraining in Digitalis not only increases a person's chances on the job market; it's also about giving people direction in their own lives.

CHAPTER 7

The customer is not the king; he's the emperor

How do we reinvent business?

A few years ago, during a break while attending a workshop on digital transformation I had the chance to speak with the CEO of a large bank. We were next to the coffee machine discussing "coffee break culture" in companies. We talked about the importance of taking the time to savor a good cup of coffee with colleagues, and we agreed that such gatherings generate better ideas than formal meetings. A bit later he reached the conclusion: "we serve very bad coffee to our employees and then we're surprised that they're not motivated." He had not immediately thought this through, because unlike other workers, management had a nice, expensive espresso machine. A few days later, he decided to install more inviting coffee corners in his business. This was the beginning of a new approach and of a new business culture. The company needed it to face the digital age. In a knowledge-based economy, companies will not be sufficiently equipped to face the future unless they treat their employees as their most valuable capital.

This change of culture is necessary because we, the Digitalis consumers, have become more demanding than ever, simply because technology makes it possible. We no longer want to line up at a shop counter, instead, we want to talk with a salesperson who knows our needs before we even open our mouths. We want companies that can predict when their customers' machines will break down, and digital technology makes all of this possible. For the first time in history, the customer occupies a truly central position. The saying "the customer is king"—a hollow slogan during the industrial era—can be forgotten. From now on the golden rule is: "the customer is the emperor". That's because these days the consumer can easily switch from one vendor to another, according to what's available. "In a digital world, there are no more limits, and customers choose the best digital service offered today by digital players. Customers do not expect less," says economist Koen De Leus, author of the book *The Winners Economy*,[63] And no company escapes. We expect personal, seamless, and fast service. From large banks to telecom companies to the butcher and the local pharmacist: today they all have to think about how they can improve their services.

The whole world is an ambassador

In Digitalis, power is in the hands of consumers. Not only does technology permit the satisfaction of their most insane demands, but consumers are also much better informed. The internet allows products and their prices to be easily compared. What's more, social networks provide opportunities for consumers to express themselves. Some don't hesitate to share the bad experience they had with a product or company with the whole world. During the industrial era, this was unthinkable. At that time, customer satisfaction was a secondary concern for many companies, which concentrated on mass production in

Model T Ford production assembly line

order to manufacture the maximum number of standardized products on the assembly line and sell them as fast as possible to the maximum number of customers. The automotive sector is a good example of this. In the past, manufacturers were more focused on selling as many cars at as low a cost as possible rather than worrying about what their customers wanted. An extreme and famous example is Henry Ford's maxim that any customer could have a car painted any color so long as it was black.

But today the consumer expects more, and certain brands have got the message. For example, if you buy a Mini these days, you can choose from an almost infinite range of options. The customers have a very sophisticated configuration tool available that allows them to totally personalize their cars. Today, digitalization of the production process has made it possible to do this job for the price of a standard product. This demonstrates how the principles of the digital economy have managed to penetrate into the core of the most traditional sectors.

Successful digital businesses are those that have been concerned with the wishes of users or end customers since the beginning. At this level, Apple's founder Steve Jobs' obsession is legendary. "Mr. Jobs was different because he was not an engineer—and that was his great strength. Instead he was obsessed with product design and aesthetics, and with making advanced technology simple to use. He repeatedly took an existing but half-formed idea—the mouse-driven computer, the digital music player, the smartphone, the tablet computer—and showed the rest of the industry how to do it properly. Rival firms scrambled to follow where he led. In the process he triggered upheavals in computing, music, telecoms and the news business that were painful for incumbent firms but welcomed by millions of consumers."[64] as one could read in the October 2011 edition of *The Economist*, published after the death of Steve Jobs. The customer experience was central and nothing would stop him. If it turned out that users systematically clicked on the wrong icon or pressed the wrong button on the keyboard, it was not because the user was clumsy (as a traditional industrial company would undoubtedly think), but because the app was not sufficiently user-friendly and would have had to be modified. Google applies the same principle: when users make a typing mistake, the search engine must recognize the intended word and suggest the correct spelling. If a user doesn't speak a website's language, the browser must be able to translate the web page into another language. It's a subtle but important change in the approach to users and customers.

It's precisely this approach that explains the success of Coolblue, a Dutch online business that has become one of the most popular webshops in the Netherlands and in Belgium. To achieve this result, you need more than a customer service with friendly employees. Anyone who buys a washing machine from Coolblue knows that their old machine will be picked up and the new one installed perfectly, which removes a thorn in the side of many buyers. The company examined which configuration was expected by buyers of new laptops, then asked manufacturers to deliver computers with precisely this configuration. And this strategy has paid off: in 2016, turnover increased by 55% to reach €857 million.[65] "The customer is king. It sounds simple, but in reality this implies that customer service must be accessible from very early in the morning to very late at night, and that what is ordered today will be delivered the next day, and sometimes on the same day. [...] To be a good online store, it's not enough to be successful in one field. You have to be excellent in everything. [...] When a customer calls, you leave with a negative score of 1-0, because it's likely that something does not meet his expectations. So you have to do everything to turn his problem into a positive experience, by resorting to some humor or a commercial courtesy," says the CEO and co-founder Peter Zwart[66], who is totally obsessed with the Net Promotor Score (or NPS). This is a customer satisfaction indicator that reflects the extent to which clients recommend your business to their friends and colleagues. The score can vary between -100 and +100. A positive NPS is considered good, a score above 50 is excellent.[67] The NPS of Coolblue was 67 in 2016. The online business is not only concerned about customer satisfaction, but also wants to make each one of them a true ambassador for the company.

A company
with a mission

For businesses, this customer focus is the new way of garnering profits. In the digital world, the starting point is not profit, but the customer. The companies whose sole ambition is to maximize their profits will sooner or later make decisions prejudicial to clients. In the long run, they pay the price. Attempts to reduce costs at all costs in order to retain margins often result in a decline in the ability to innovate or in the quality of the service. Successful companies have a mission that goes beyond simple profitability. For example, Google's mission is to organize all information available around the world and make it universally accessible and usable by all. Apple's first mission was "to make a contribution to the world by developing tools for the minds that advance humanity." At Coolblue, the mission is to ensure that customers "are happy thanks to the purchase."

Businesses that sincerely believe in their mission make every decision according to this mission, which changes the company DNA. The main goal shifts from profitability or value for the shareholder to the development of innovative products, the design of new services, or the optimization of user-friendliness. This is exactly what can make the difference between your company and its competitors. For example, customer focus can paradoxically be the best way to succeed, and even to reap larger benefits. This explains why many internet companies start by offering their products or services for free. It allows them not only to quickly conquer an important share of the market, but at the same time they also receive a lot more feedback on their product or service. The engineers can then develop the necessary improvements with which to win over more customers or users by offering them a better product. It's only when this is all in place that the paid products or services can be subsequently developed, allowing the company to earn revenue. Thanks to this recipe, Facebook and Google have become companies that generate billions of dollars in profits.

I don't think that every company with a clear mission will become an international giant. But on the other hand, a well-defined mission can give a business a new boost and get it back on track. We have already seen this type of transformation in Belgium. Until the banking crisis of 2011, Belfius was a traditional bank. Like all other players in the financial sector, the bank (at the time called Dexia) concentrated especially on profitability and value creation for its shareholders. The share price was more important than the satisfaction rate of customers and the pursuit of profit eventually took on pathological dimensions. Dexia was finally overwhelmed by the banking crisis and went under. It was fully dismantled and the healthy parts were renamed Belfius. Under the guidance of the new CEO, Marc Raisiere, the bank has totally reinvented itself. Its mission has been redefined, abandoning its role as a profit machine, to become an important link in financing the Belgian economy. In any healthy economy banks play a crucial role, using surpluses derived from household savings to provide credit to young entrepreneurs, well-established companies, public authorities, and hospitals. Moreover, the priority given to customer satisfaction has become one of the pillars in the resurrection of Belfius. The bank has launched major advertising campaigns to explain, not only to its customers, but also to its employees and contractors, that the customer was its primary concern. Result: customer satisfaction has increased (according to the figures published by the bank, 95% of customers are satisfied)[68], as well as the net profit (535 million euros in 2016). Belfius employees have rediscovered their pride.

Happy employees

At present, the societal mission of companies is still much more important than innovation: if their employees are passionate individuals who understand the objectives and mission of the company, the innovations will follow. This presupposes a perfect match between the company's culture and its mission. It's not credible to aim for high customer satisfaction if employees work in an uncomfortable environment using obsolete equipment—and machines that serve bad coffee. This type of environment will not motivate employees, even when they must ensure that customers are satisfied and stay so. Employees are the main capital of a business, especially today, as we move towards a knowledge-based economy. Companies must therefore pamper and nourish that human capital. A good number of them are busy restructuring to become future proof—in other words, equipped to deal with the future—because they now understand the need for responsiveness. But all of them haven't yet understood that their future will not depend solely on their products and services, but also on their ability to make their company culture evolve in concert with the new age.

Employees are the main capital of a business, especially today, as we move towards a knowledge-based economy.

Proximus, the main telecom provider in Belgium, is a good example of the importance of developing a healthy company culture. It has seen its turnover drop year by year as a result of telecom market saturation. Former CEO Didier Bellens thought he could find a solution by cutting costs and investing less than other telecommunications companies, in order to provide a stable dividend for the Belgian State. The current CEO Dominique Leroy has faced a major challenge since taking up her position. She made it clear that it was absurd to think that Proximus could not grow further. She made a clean sweep and put growth back on the corporate menu. Her initiatives were applauded. "Unlike Bellens, Leroy is backed by her 13,000 employees. Thanks to fluid and open communication, she put an end to Bellens' reign of terror. She ensured that all staff share a common goal: to make Proximus a more flexible and creative company. These changes helped Proximus to post in 2014—for the first time in a long time— an increase in both its turnover and profits, and this was done two years ahead of schedule," as reported in the Flemish daily *De Tijd* in 2017.[69] This shows the importance of an inspiring project in our digital world. CEOs can achieve great things, provided they are a source of inspiration for their employees.

Openness is the first essential success factor if we want employees to be enthusiastic about the company's mission. Managers must be accessible and share the problems of the company with all employees. When the workers spend eight hours or more in the office, they have at least the right to know what they're doing, why they're doing it, and for whom.

The second success factor is flexibility. During the industrial era, workers were subjected to very strict controls to ensure successful completion of the tasks given to them. This explains why the companies installed time clocks: according to the logic of the industrial era, every one had to start and end work at the same time, even if we know that not everyone is at their best at the same time (there are "morning people" and there are "evening people"), and that the imposed work schedule doesn't always align with the necessities imposed by private life (nothing is more frustrating than rigid schedules for those who have to struggle each day to arrive on time or face traffic jams). According to the time clock principle, presence is more important than the quality of the work done. Companies will still need managers in the digital era, but they will no longer fulfill a purely controlling function. Trust has replaced control. Good managers are responsible for their employees and ensure that they can carry out their work, just like a coach would. They don't impose a way of doing things, but ensure that everyone has access to the right people, the right opportunities, and the necessary resources. Without good managers, things won't work. This is the error that Google made in 2000 when they suppressed all management functions and eliminated any form of hierarchy within the company. After a few weeks, the experiment was terminated because of the chaos it caused.

The third success factor is diversity and inclusion. Companies from the industrial era are typically male bastions with few women near the top of the hierarchy. In 2016 only 14 of the 350 largest European companies had a female CEO.[70] Yet diversity increases the success rate. Google has tested this by assembling three very different teams and giving them the same mission. The first team consisted only of men of comparable age and education. The second team consisted of an equally homogeneous group of women, while the third group was made up of an equal number of men and women of different ages and cultural backgrounds. The results? The homogeneous groups were faster and found a solution very quickly. This is not surprising. All members of the group quickly agreed because they shared the same norms and values. Things were more difficult in the heterogeneous group, and the discussions were more demanding. But in the end, this group's solution proved to be the better one. Those who share the same opinions quickly think that they have the right solution, and they don't consider other possibilities. That's why they only listen to some of their clients, namely those whose world-view best fits their frame of reference and their values. A company's clientele is not so homogeneous. It includes people of different kinds, ages, cultures and religions. Businesses inevitably make mistakes if they ignore these differences when making important decisions. Enriching human capital and encouraging the development of an open culture represents a major challenge, both for large companies and for traditional ones, but also for start-ups and trendy tech companies. Even the latter sometimes find it difficult to implement this fundamental principle of the digital economy. The innovative Uber platform has changed the way of moving millions of people, but at the same time, it allowed a clearly macho culture to develop within its ranks, leading to a series of scandals, dissatisfaction among employees, and finally the exodus of quality people. Amazon has fundamentally changed the way we do our purchases and became a real juggernaut. The fact remains that the company regularly makes the headlines because of its rigid corporate culture and difficult working conditions in its warehouses. This shows that in this area, even digital businesses still have a long way to go.

The right
to fail

Darwin's law also applies to businesses: it's not the biggest ones that survive, but those with the greatest ability to adapt. That's why it's essential to give employees sufficient maneuvering room to experiment, and to allow them to fail. Both are inseparable. If some people never fail, it's probably because they have not tried out enough things. Many European companies are going to have to learn to live with this change of mentality. We tend to spend two years thinking about a new application, anticipating all possible problems, two more years developing the project, so that we can finally launch a product that has been completely surpassed. In an era where new technologies follow one another at dizzying speeds, we cannot allow ourselves this luxury. It's only by experimenting that creativity can flourish, and in the end this always leads to the development of better products. It's better to launch a product or service quickly, be alert for feedback from users, and apply the necessary corrections as soon as possible. Not all projects, nor all Google projects, will turn into a global success. The best known example is the Google Glass, a portable PC in the shape of eyeglasses, which was removed from the consumer market, even though today it's undergoing a revival for professional applications, especially in the logistics and health care sectors.

Still, a failure can have a positive impact in the long term. The experience of a previous failure can often turn into a success factor in a new project. Before smartphones appeared, Google launched a service in the U.S. whereby users could call to obtain the results of their online queries. It was a flop. Google, however, retained a large audio database of keywords spoken with the different American accents. Today this data constitutes the foundation of voice search, a way of executing Google searches with voice commands.

Creativity is, paradoxically, stimulated by limits. Large companies still think that the best innovations come when dozens or even hundreds of engineers think together. This generates very top-heavy structures, excessive and excessively costly, and it rarely leads to the development of better products. In fact, employees will only truly kindle their creativity when placed in small teams that have to deal with constraints. At Google, the development teams have very limited means, which compels them to come up with creative solutions. It's no coincidence that Gmail, Google's email service—which has more than one billion users—was developed by a single engineer. In 2001, Paul Buchheit created the first version of Gmail, repurposing the code taken from an old project. He put it together in almost one day. The following months and years were devoted to fine-tuning. Google employees quickly used Gmail for internal mail, and Google didn't make their webmail available to the public until 2004. At that time, only a dozen people were still working on the project.[71]

The same happened with Android, the mobile operating system launched by Google in 2007. At Google, only nine people worked on the project. They were in competition with Nokia, then the world's number one in the field of mobile telephony. At the time, more than one in three mobile phones was a Nokia. At the Finnish company, hundreds of engineers worked on the Symbian project, Nokia's own operating system. The small Google team released a creative solution based on open-source software. This source code, accessible to all for free, made it possible to quickly complete the project. The result was better and more user-friendly. In spite of this, Nokia stuck to its own closed operating system. Symbian ended up being completely wiped off the map when Google released relatively cheap Android devices. Nokia lost its leadership position and was absorbed by Microsoft in 2014.

Small is the new big

Limited resources stimulate creativity, which is good news for start-ups and small businesses. It has never been so easy to become an entrepreneur. Previously, to launch your business, you had to start by investing thousands of euros for computers and servers. Today, a laptop costs a few hundred euros and the cloud gives you access to virtually unlimited storage capacity and incredible computing power. Digitalization projects us into a world where young entrepreneurs with meager capital can immediately compete against the existing giants. Starters have opportunities that their predecessors could barely dream of. They are already flexible and can start their project at full speed. They still lack money and customers, but have fantastic ideas. They often find themselves up to their necks in difficulties, but have an incredible survival instinct that drives them to the extreme. It's no coincidence that young companies with just a few employees more and more frequently outdo the larger players.

It's never been so easy to become an entrepreneur.

Many large, well-established companies often struggle to adopt the same flexibility as startups. This is because they have relied for years on the same products to ensure their profitability, and have never felt the need to innovate. They have set up huge structures with the sole objective of producing the same thing at a lower cost. As a result, they are tempted to ignore the changes underway and to think that their operational model will still be relevant.

This is why car manufacturers are now at the crossroads, because for years they have only been concerned with competitors in their sector, and have totally ignored the activities of digital companies like Google and Uber in the development of autonomous cars. They were also surprised by Tesla, which started producing electric vehicles from scratch, revolutionizing the entire market. The result: the traditional manufacturers have had to recognize that they were surpassed in the field of technology by actors they had totally ignored.

There are many ways to catch up. Large companies are increasingly trying to integrate with other companies and start-ups in vast ecosystems, so that they do not miss out on the latest technological developments. They've modified their organizations, simplifying their hierarchical structures and creating separate entities authorized to experiment without restriction. Sometimes they collaborate with their clients, in order to come up with solutions that they had not yet imagined or that they felt they could not achieve on their own. In the end, we come back to the same principle: keep being a big company while using the formulas of small businesses—this isn't always easy. Do you remember Kodak? This American company was once the world number one in the photography business. In 1888, Kodak developed the first roll of film usable in daylight, and the company launched the first camera for the general public. Many innovations catapulted Kodak into a monopolistic position in the American amateur photography market. In fact, Kodak had made the wrong strategic choices, but was still able to maintain its dominant position for a long time. "In 1975, Kodak invented the first digital camera, but it decided not to pursue its development, for fear of losing some of the huge profits made in the analog photography market. Kodak made the same mistake in the 1990s. Despite multibillion dollar investments in the development of photo technology, mobile phones, and other digital devices, the company left this sector to competitors like Canon and Sony, still out of fear of undermining the profits from its analog division," reported the Dutch daily *NRC Handelsblad* in 2012 after Kodak—which was on the verge of bankruptcy—filed for chapter 11 bankruptcy protection status in the U.S.[72]

The tech company Apple succeeded where Kodak stumbled. It entered the technological race at the crucial moment and systematically moved in different directions. The company has been operating since 1976. At first, it was just a computer manufacturer, which had managed to conquer the world with its famous Macintosh. In 2001, Apple launched its iPod music player, which totally revolutionized the music industry. And in 2007, it introduced the iPhone, which really marked the breakthrough of the smartphone, a device that is now an integral part of our daily lives. In fact, Apple never launched the first computer, MP3 player, or smartphone on the market. However, this American tech company has always managed to turn these new products into commercial successes.

It's, moreover, a preconceived idea that only technology companies can open radically new paths. The Solvay chemical group has been in existence since 1863, and in the course of more than 150 years, it has reinvented itself several times. Its founder Ernest Solvay conceived back then a new process for manufacturing sodium carbonate. But since then, his company has turned into a group specializing in chemistry and producing composite materials for the aerospace industry. Another example is Umicore. The company was established in 1906 under the name Union Miniere, a group that for decades controlled the exploitation of raw materials in the Congo. Today, the group has become a high-tech materials company, specializing in the recycling of precious metals and in the production of materials for rechargeable batteries intended especially for electric cars. These two champions are among the world leaders in their fields, and both have a market value of more than 10 billion euros, which proves that companies older than 100 years also have a future, as long as they manage to reinvent themselves.

CHAPTER 8

No more lines at the checkout

How do we reinvent shopping?

In Digitalis, your "local" store is located in China or Amsterdam. With just a few clicks, you can access an almost infinite range of products at incredibly low prices. You make most of your purchases online, and you only go to the store to compare products and get advice; digital media has become the most important factor in your buying decisions. Of course, you can still go shopping in real stores, but children's diapers and beverages are automatically ordered by smart devices, and delivered the next day to your home. You don't hesitate to order five pairs of sneakers, even if you only intend to keep one of them. Why? Because it's possible. The shopping experience in Digitalis isn't an illusion; we've already come most of the way. In recent years, the digital evolution has already profoundly changed our purchasing habits. We are no longer satisfied with a mediocre or impersonal service, because thanks to our computer and our smartphone, we have alternative solutions. As a result, stores must also reinvent themselves.

In the future, we will only go to the shops if the experience is really worth it. In Digitalis, we are entitled to the *crème de la crème*.

A fascinating period
for commerce

Online commerce is not new. We've been able to make internet purchases since the mid-90s. In the beginning, they were small purchases, like books, CDs, or concert tickets, and they remained very limited. That era is over. Today, online shopping is an integral part of our daily lives. Respectable brands and stores can no longer afford not to have their own webshop. For a specific purchase, consumers can always go to the store to get more information, so that they can subsequently place an order in the shop or the webshop that has the best offer. Conversely, it's possible to compare prices online before going to a store. When you know the product and know who the best vendor is, it's simple to order it online without getting up from your chair. The result of this online commerce (or internet economy) is that our roads are now overrun by transport company vans delivering parcels to customers.

The history of online commerce is a beautiful metaphor for the break between the last two industrial revolutions and the digital transformation that we know today. Up until the mid-50s, we shopped exclusively at the local grocery store. One couldn't imagine a closer proximity: the grocer knew your preferences, and buying experiences were personalized and pleasant. But because of their small size, those shops were quite expensive and had limited selection. One had to wait a long time before new products were stocked. Industrialization created not only the assembly line but also supermarkets, those large spaces where customers could serve themselves and pay for their purchases at the cash register. Supermarkets were established in the United States during the First World War. The retail sector subsequently adopted the industrial concepts: large space, low price, and broad choice. The other side of the coin is the lack of personal service, friendliness, and personalized advice.

Digitalization offers the best of both worlds: the grocer's personal service combined with the bountiful offering and low prices of the supermarket. All these elements are present in the online shop at a more impressive scale and with ultrafast delivery. Thanks to the computerization of customer data, webshops are able to identify us. Customers who visit Amazon's online store all have a different homepage. For the customers of the online bookstore, the books are in first position on screen, while those who regularly buy sporting goods have a home page offering these products. Online stores can respond in a customized way to the needs of each customer, based on their buying behavior— for example, based on the products they buy most often or on which they click regularly. Combined with artificial intelligence, this opens the door to personalized recommendations.

Well-organized online stores "recognize" their customers immediately. If you visit a site for the second time, you are immediately connected and hosted in your own language. The store has your address and payment preferences. It's practical, simple, and personal. And it doesn't stop there: thanks to artificial intelligence, your supermarket's online store could analyze your preferences. The webshop will immediately know which are your favorite vegetables, the fact that you dislike fish, or that you are allergic to cow's milk. Based on this information, the supermarket could offer you a personalized menu every week. In reality, this approach is not the same as social contact, even if you recall

Digitalization offers the best of both worlds: the grocer's personal service combined with the bountiful offering and low prices of the supermarket.

that in recent years, social contact has continually decreased in many chain stores.

E-commerce has started a movement like a pendulum swing: we shop less often for purchases that require little or no social contact, but at the same time, we need more stores for human contact and advice. These types stores will be better able to survive the digital transformation than those that are just large impersonal spaces.

For traditional stores, the bar has now been set very high, because successful webshops are totally obsessed with the need to make your life easier. Whatever the app, the starting point is always to provide the users with an optimal experience. The search for the optimal spot for each icon is almost obsessive and all the intermediate steps between finding the right product and payment method are optimized. But not all sites have the same level of quality. Often I still encounter webshops with endless and complex lists of products. They discourage visitors instead of urging them to buy. It's no coincidence that the most popular webshops like Amazon, Zalando, Sale-Exclusive, or Decathlon have perfected the online experience.

In addition to the convenience, speed is a fundamental pillar of online commerce. We've gotten used to the idea that we can order today and receive our products at home the next day. Deliveries are also possible during the weekend, which was unthinkable until recently. We are amazingly spoiled. Better still: we, as consumers, have regained power. Twenty years ago, we had no choice and had to go to the only accessible store, and had to accept the delivery deadlines set by the vendor if a product was not immediately available. Today, it's possible to receive the same product the next day, and choose it on the internet from the store offering the best product and the best service.

In the digital world, speed is not limited to delivery times; it also applies to websites. We expect a site to open in less than a second on a mobile device. Through measurement, Google has found that a visitor's heart rate increases sharply after waiting for more than three seconds. Many stores underestimate this mechanism. According to a Google study, a mobile site opens in 22 seconds on average. This seems like an eternity, especially if one knows that 53% of visitors leave the sites after waiting for

The consumer still takes the time to choose a product, but finds it unbearable to be slowed down by the technology.

3 seconds.[73] The consumer has become accustomed to being served very quickly, both in the physical and digital worlds. The consumer still takes the time to choose a product, but finds it unbearable to be slowed down by technology.

Another major challenge is to find the right balance between the possibilities offered by technology and the protection of private data. Online stores can only improve friendliness if they have certain visitor data. Preferences, lists of favorite products, purchase history, even geolocation: all of this data is useful for optimizing the visitor experience. A user who refuses to let a site record service-enhancing data will not be able to benefit from the same personalized approach, nor will the user always obtain access to all the services. But it's a legitimate choice that sites must respect. Companies that collect data about their customers need to have an excellent reputation and foolproof reliability. As soon as customers have the impression that their information has been handled negligently—for example, if they receive unsolicited e-mails for car loans after visiting a site which specifically offers such credit—they lose confidence. In the digital world, this type of behavior is immediately chastised.

The question of the protection of private life in our digital world is discussed in more detail in the last chapter.

The Zalando effect

When the internet first began, numerous analysts firmly believed that many products could never be sold online. Today, it's clear that e-commerce has become a reality across the board. Ten years ago, it was unthinkable to buy clothes or shoes online. Almost no one imagined doing this type of purchase without trying the goods on beforehand. But today, carriers deliver daily packages of clothes or shoes that were ordered online. This abrupt change is thanks to Zalando, the German webshop created in 2008 by Robert Gentz and David Schneider, who started selling flip-flops online from a small apartment in Berlin. They quickly noticed that virtually no one in Europe sold shoes on the internet, while the American webshop Zappos had generated a turnover of 1 billion dollars that year. The German duo had the idea of reproducing this miracle in Europe. In 2017, the company posted a turnover of 4.5 billion euros. What was the secret of their success? Zalando was able to convince hesitant consumers thanks to the principle of "free returns". Customers make a purchase, try the product at home, and then they can return it if it doesn't fit. They then get a refund for the returned item. It's thanks to this system that Zalando succeeded in convincing Europeans to purchase clothing and shoes online. Nobody had thought it possible to sell this type of product on a large scale online, until this young internet company demonstrated the opposite and forced the traditional clothing and footwear stores to offer their products online. Since then, all major brands have a well-stocked webshop, and nobody minds buying clothes online anymore.

The Zalando effect has affected all sectors. In the beginning, most companies thought that they wouldn't have to bother with online commerce—until this young company demonstrated the opposite, thereby pushing all sectors into online commerce and forcing all traditional companies to embark on the difficult process of digitalizing their industries. In the travel business, Booking.com had the effect of a tidal wave. During the emergence of online commerce, travel agencies couldn't imagine that customers would one day book their holidays via the internet. Nevertheless, this was one of the first sectors to embark on digitalization after having noticed that consumers were booking their hotels via Booking.com. We are observing the same trend in the food sector: no one had ever imagined that fresh products would be ordered via a webshop, with home delivery. But the Dutch company Takeaway, the Swedish "Lina's Matkasse" or the German HelloFresh group entered the market with their packages holding all the ingredients needed for a tasty meal, including the recipe. Many consumers seem to find the formula interesting and are ordering these packages online.

Buying abroad

A lot of chain stores are suffering from the arrival of online commerce and many have already filed for bankruptcy. In 2013, the Belgian chain Photo Hall, which sold cameras and multimedia, had to close the business, having failed to resist the onslaught of large multimedia chain stores, and having failed to switch to online business. A year later, it was the turn of the Free Record Shop, after 45 years of sales of records and CDs. The chain store had not found an adequate response to the collapse of CD sales and digitalization of the music industry. In

2017, the bankruptcy of the American toy giant "Toys'R US" caused quite a stir. Despite its 1600 stores, its 64,000 employees, and an annual turnover of around $11.5 billion, it succumbed to competition from online commerce. All these companies, which had in common the lack of a website or webshop, were swept away by these (new) competitors.

And it's paradoxical: while consumers have resolutely adopted online shopping, many merchants continue to hesitate.

But the products or services once offered by these chains still exist; we've never listened to so much music or taken so many photos. And smartphones are an integral part of our daily lives, most of us have grown up with them. The defunct chains didn't see the changes coming. They missed the digitalization boat and lost their market position.

These experiences must force all stores to think, because many chain stores have waited too long before switching to online business.

European companies should recognize the potential to sell their products to the 4 billion consumers that are one click away from their shops. And that's also true for SME's. Luckily, thousands of entrepreneurs have started to sell abroad thanks to the internet. An example that surprised me is DMLights, a small lighting company with one shop, in Heist-op-den-Berg. The founder's son challenged his father to start a digital business some years ago. His father was not expecting any success from this at the beginning. But the tenacity of the son led to a successful business that is now representing 70% of overall business. Thanks to their webshop, they expanded from 35 to 100 employees, including 6 in China, to foster their sales with Alibaba.

Good for the budget, bad for the environment?

The popularity of e-commerce, however, has a negative impact on the environment, because of the flood of delivery people making trips. Now that consumers have tasted the ease offered by online shopping, it would be unthinkable to pull back. Consumers want to continue buying online and to receive their purchases as quickly as possible. It's clear that we are still in a transition phase and that e-commerce must go through its growing pains for which we still have to find solutions. The use of new technology always starts with chaos and inefficiency, which can be resolved at a later stage. For e-commerce, the main challenge will be to optimize the underlying logistics system. The increased use of electric vehicles for parcel delivery could help reduce the environmental footprint, while improved transportation systems would reduce the number of missed deliveries (forcing re-deliveries the next day). Here too, new small-scale technology companies are offering solutions. I am thinking of deliveries by drones or faster solutions, such as the bike couriers from Parcify, a delivery company founded in 2015. The start-up has developed an application that organizes the delivery of an online order using the geolocation of the customer's smartphone rather than a fixed address. Result: the parcels are always delivered to where the customer is. You can probably also see their bike couriers when you jog in the park, or when enjoying a drink on a bar's terrace. This approach is of significant interest to delivery companies. At the end of 2017, Parcify was also bought by BPost. Meanwhile, other alternatives are emerging. In another example from 2016, BPost created, together with Bringr, a parcel delivery platform with the deliveries done by private individuals. This was inspired by other examples of the collaborative economy, such as Airbnb and Uber. With Bringr, everyone can become a courier. If a parcel is to be transported from Brussels to Liege, and you happen to go to Liege, then you can take charge of the parcel and deliver it for a fee. I am also thinking of Bringme, which rents lockers to which you can have your orders delivered. Today, there are nearly 750 companies and buildings equipped with smart Bringme lockers, where it's possible to have your parcel delivered or exchanged.[74] Google is experimenting with project Wing, an autonomous delivery drone service that aims to increase access to goods, reduce traffic congestion in cities, and help ease the CO_2 emissions attributable to the transportation of goods. And in the United States, Amazon has just launched its in-house delivery, in other words, the delivery into your home. Via Amazon Key, the couriers have access to your dwelling and deposit the package in the entrance hall. A smart lock and a camera keep the process under control.

Google is experimenting with Wing, a delivery drone.

Shopping
with your GPS

Online commerce has raised the bar for traditional stores. On-line boutiques have really spoiled us. It's possible to place an order via the computer, to compare prices, to obtain product information, and to view video recommendations, and then everything will be delivered tomorrow! Contrary to general expectations, the service offered by traditional stores is less personalized than that offered online. From now on, stores will have to offer that little bit extra that will make the difference—and technology can help them. For example, IKEA's after sales service has been adapted to the digital reality. If you have to replace you IKEA closet hinges, you can order them for free via their internet site. Moreover, the brand has launched an app that allows you to choose a sofa and see if it fits in your living room thanks to augmented reality. Customers will then know immediately which sofa (and which color) will best suit their interior. For customers this is an entirely new experience: they can wander through the shop trying out different sofas, and immediately virtually transport the sofas to their homes in order to visualize the whole scene via the app.

The possibilities of indoor GPS technology are also very promising. Thanks to a GPS app installed on your smartphone, you can easily locate a shop assistant or the product you're looking for. Moreover, you can take a photo, for example of a screw, and the application will tell you the exact place where it's located in the DIY store.

For chain stores, it can be tempting to equip their outlets with a maximum number of technological gadgets, but it's rarely the right way to create quality; the real challenges are in adopting the technology that will bring real added value to customers. For a furniture store, it will be augmented reality; for a supermarket, contactless payments will be a plus; and a clothing store can add an extra dimension to their level of service by allowing customers to share photos of themselves wearing different outfits on social networks, or to choose another outfit using touch screens in the dressing rooms, and ask the sales assistant to bring them other models or sizes. Finally, the real issue is more about the customer experience, and less about technology. Result: the demarcations between the traditional and virtual stores will blur. Some chain stores are struggling to get started, while others have a good understanding of the issues. A.S. Adventure is a good example of this. Previously, if the desired product wasn't available in a store, you would go home empty-handed. At best, you could try again a few days later, hoping that in the meantime the product had been delivered. Today, if you can't immediately buy your item, an employee orders it via the webshop, and you have it delivered to your home the next day for free. In the past, it was unthinkable: the stores were only concerned with their commission and even considered their own webshops to be competitors. This change in mindset prevents the chain from losing customers. The sale is simply transferred from one channel to another. Lens-Online, the online shop for contact lenses is another example: it works with opticians who act as a pick-up point. The brand also offers the best of both worlds: the consumer buys less expensive contact lenses while benefiting from the expertise of a professional in case of a problem, or simply for advice. This model is called *omnichannel* and represents the future for chain stores.

The supermarket
of the future

In supermarkets, we'll soon see what the stores of the future will look like. Up to now supermarkets were never very appealing: you choose from among thousands of products, you put everything in a cart and then head for the checkout where you yourself have to empty the cart onto the checkout counter conveyor belt and, in most European grocery stores, you also put all of your items in bags as soon as they're scanned. This means that when the cashier starts scanning the goods the race against the clock begins—you have to keep up with the cashier's frenetic pace, putting everything into bags as fast as possible. When you're done, you pull out your wallet, insert your debit card into the terminal, and enter your secret code. This is anything but a pleasant experience, and may soon change with the arrival of the internet giants on the retail scene.

The internet giant Amazon launched a bombshell into the world of superstores by buying the American grocery store chain Whole Foods in 2017 for the tidy sum of 14 billion dollars. The fact that Amazon is entering this domain as a direct competitor of traditional supermarkets has even made investors nervous, and has caused the stock price of practically all distribution groups to drop. Amazon's initiative has unleashed a tidal wave in the wholesale distribution business, where, until recently, the different chains only had to worry about their direct competitors. Shortly after the takeover of Whole Foods, the US supermarket chain Walmart and Google concluded an agreement. Walmart announced that it would not only sell hundreds of thousands of articles via Google's shopping tool, but that it would also be possible to order a daily basket of everyday products via the *Google Home Smart Speaker*. In the near future,

American consumers will be able to ask their Smart Speaker to order a two pounds of potatoes, two heads of cauliflower, and some sausage—all of which will be delivered to them a few hours later. Chinese internet giant Alibaba has again invested 2.5 billion euros in the Sun Art Retail Group, the second largest supermarket chain in China.[75]

Traditional stores aren't dead; if they were the internet companies wouldn't be investing in them.

Traditional stores aren't dead; if they were, the internet companies wouldn't be investing in them. Companies like Amazon and Alibaba will reinvent the stores and have the client retake his place at the center of the process, using the latest technologies.

Amazon Go is described as a store where you never have to wait.

We can already glean some information from Amazon Go to find out what the future supermarket will look like. Amazon Go is the pilot store opened by the internet giant in 2016 in the city of Seattle in the western United States. The store opened to the public in early 2018. At the entrance, customers scan a QR code with their smartphone and are thereafter immediately followed by cameras in the store's shelves, which record the products customer's drop into their carts.

Then at checkout, everything is automatically calculated and charged through their Amazon account. Customers no longer have to scan the products or take out their debit cards. Amazon Go is described as a store where you never have to wait. This system will become the norm in the future, to the extent that the internet giants will have made supermarkets—with whom they are now competing—their new playground.

In China, the internet giant jd.com, competitor of the giant online store Alibaba, opened a supermarket at the close of last year that has no staff, which also uses cameras, facial recognition, and artificial intelligence to record all customer movements and the products they take from the shelves. The company is also considering a delivery service using driverless cars.[76]

The detractors of this system predict major layoffs of supermarket employees. But other avenues can be followed. These days, the role of the checkout attendant is limited to scanning the products and registering the payment. With technology, this step will disappear, but supermarkets could employ people to wait for the customers, advise them about certain products, and make suggestions for the evening meal. This would be a return to the more personal relationship one had at the local grocer a few decades ago. Customers will probably be willing to travel for this type of experience.

Your salesperson:
artificial intelligence

In the digital era, brands and stores will no longer be able to advertise as they did in the past. Advertising today has to be absolutely relevant. You don't want to see advertising for diapers while watching a movie. On the other hand, you would be glad to receive car ads as soon as you start considering a replacement for your own vehicle. Advertisements will have to conform to consumers' mental worlds. This challenge is much more difficult than many companies think.

But note that we are inseparable from our smartphones. Conclusion: we are permanently reachable. It's precisely this availability that should make marketing specialists more thoughtful about the relevance of their message in relation to the moment when they send it. Advertisements issued via Facebook are a good example. No one is interested in mincemeat ads when they are reading their friends' posts. These ads are counterproductive because they irritate their readers. If you're in the middle of preparing a party for your friends, you would probably be more open to ads for fancy clothes or champagne. Or, if you were about to buy a house, you would probably welcome mortgage proposals appearing on your screen. This hyper-personalized approach is possible in the digital era, given the fact that the whole world leaves behind digital traces, which artificial intelligence is quite capable of analyzing. At the technological level, it's not difficult to identify and record who stops to study an online advertisement and to subsequently adapt the advertising to the collected data.

The next step for merchants will be to use artificial intelligence to sell ... artificial intelligence. In the United States, smart speakers are gradually making inroads into the daily lives of citizens. We've already mentioned that these devices not only have all kinds of uses in the home, they could also be used to place orders. This evolution will force manufacturers to use artificial intelligence, not only to reach consumers at the right moment, but also to have them come under the radar of the artificial intelligence lurking in their devices (e.g. smartphones), which will be increasingly used for making purchases. If a consumer wants to buy a new coat, these devices should make several recommendations. The more a product appears near the top of the list of recommendations, the greater the probability of its purchase.

The brands and stores will have to develop new strategies for retaining customer loyalty, because here too, the old formulas are out of step. Take the "loyalty card": it no longer encourages customers to be loyal to a store, and we may even doubt if this has ever been the case. In reality, each supermarket issues its own loyalty card, and all of them offer the same advantages, so that they are all interchangeable in the end. No card makes a customer loyal to a supermarket. Things could be different if this card provided exclusive benefits—for example automatic scanning of products and payment without waiting at the checkout.

If there are arguments to which we have become very receptive they are those related to convenience and friendliness. Amazon's Dash Button is a good example of the new strategies. For more than 300 products, Amazon provides a small device that consists of nothing more than a simple button. As soon as you activate it, you send a buy signal for a given product. You can, for example, stick one of these Dash Buttons on your washing machine and push it when you need to buy laundry detergent. You can also stick one in your bathroom, which will allow you to order toothpaste with a single touch. Your product will then be delivered to you the following day without any further intervention on your part, and all of your purchases will be automatically billed. These new technologies and applications should greatly simplify your life. In Digitalis, we'll be able to deliver heaps of products very easily to your home. But we'll keep going to stores. No longer out of necessity, but just to have a good time.

CHAPTER 9

A financial manager for everyone

How can we reinvent banks
and insurance?

When I was little, my mother would often take me to the post office, where we had to stand in line to get cash. Things had already
improved by the time I was a student: every week, I stood at the
counter at the bank to make a cash withdrawal. Today, I don't
have to stand in line. Only very rarely do I withdraw cash, because I pay for practically all my purchases with a debit card, and
increasingly I pay with my smartphone. In the future, young
people will probably no longer be using cards or cash. This is the
result of a long process of digitalizing money, something that has
simplified our financial transactions enormously. With the current state of technology, we are pretty much able to manage our
money the way millionaires do. A lot of progress has been made
over the years. It won't be much longer before we can manage our
finances from our living rooms, or we can pay invoices or buy
shares on the stock market by ordering a digital financial assistant to do so via voice command. Furthermore, reinventing the
European financial sector creates economic opportunities.

Non-identified digitalization

Digitalization improves the comfort level of its users. The best example is the simplicity with which we manage our finances. Today, financial management is handled without any human contact: the money is transferred from one account to another, and you pay for your purchases with your card, smartphone, or with one click for online purchases. In a certain sense, for the last ten years we've been managing our money the same way we've been treating our vacation pictures and private documents more recently: we don't keep them ourselves, instead we store them digitally in a secured place that we can access any time we want. For several years, nobody has been keeping all of their savings in cash. So, it's a little strange that we are still cautious when it comes to the digital revolution, when our money—which, despite everything, represents one of the most important aspects of our material lives—has been digitalized and transformed at incredible speed since the creation of electronic bank accounts in the 1980s.

The early dematerialization (or digitalization) of money—which is the most important resource of banks—means that banks have been able to digitalize their key activities since the beginning of the internet. And, they did so in a very constructive way. The internet had been expanding since the early 1990s, and just five years later it became possible to make bank transactions from your home or via online banking through the bank's internet website in many countries. It was no longer necessary to visit an office or make phone calls to your bank. Before the end of the 90s, the majority of banks had developed genuine internet strategies, and in the early 2000s, we witnessed the opening of the first completely online banks. Created in 2002, Keytrade Bank was the first online bank in Belgium. From this moment on, it has been possible to manage our money via a bank without a physical office. Today, online banks have become the standard. The banks that don't get there, will probably fail. This shows just how much progress the banking sector has made since the start of digitalization. This also proves that digitalization is not like a tsunami that has wiped entire sectors off the map. Despite extensive digitalization, banks remain fruitful organizations, but they must closely follow the digital evolution. "Digitalization is a progressive process, which we can compare to global warming, of which one of the consequences is rising water levels. There are banks that find themselves on the dunes and others are on the dyke. The bank of the future is on the dyke. Because we don't know for how much longer the dunes will exist," explains Max Jadot, CEO of BNP Paribas Fortis.[77]

The financial manager

As a result of the early dematerialization of money, banks are a step ahead of many other companies when it comes to digitalization. They have also rapidly implemented the transition towards mobile phones. Mobile phone technologies didn't really take off until 2007, with the launch of the first iPhone. Four years later, the banking sector already had 100,000 subscribers to mobile banking in Belgium, and in 2016, this number had increased to 4.5 million subscribers.[78]

In a certain sense, banks were forced to quickly jump on the mobile phone bandwagon. Until the banking crisis of 2007 and 2008, they had completely ignored their central mission of

providing services to customers, of guaranteeing payment traffic, and of providing the opportunity for the economy to stabilize by enabling savings to be turned into loans. Until 2007, they
were mainly focused on speculating, increasing their balance
sheets and helping shareholders. Banks were much less concerned with the quality of their services. The banking crisis
caused a breach of trust, and financial institutions were forced
to do everything in their power to restore and improve the quality of their services. They've largely succeeded. Today, just
downloading your bank's app makes it possible to pay in stores
with your smartphone or to split a restaurant bill between
friends and pay for your share in real time. Similarly, the app
enables you to get answers to your questions at any moment of
the day. The digital evolution has made it possible to put the client at the heart of the process with quick, high-quality service.
For the first time in years, people once again feel positive about
banking services. According to the director of KBC, Johan Thijs,
the fast digitalization of the banking sector wasn't imposed by
the need to save costs. "We did it because we were confronted
with the evolution of our customers' needs, new technologies,
and the increase of online competition in all our key markets.
We want to increase our revenues by at least 2.25% per year.
That's why we have to diversify. In particular, it's possible to sell
insurance and investment products through digital channels.
But we have to use digitalization to our advantage by improving
efficiency, which we don't want to deprive ourselves of." Since
the launch of the app for mobile phones, KBC has been selling
two-thirds of their direct loans through digital channels.[79]

Mobile banking and payment apps are just a foretaste of what
is to come. Banks are sitting on enormous amounts of data that
have huge potential. A bank can easily find out whether a client
pays more for their energy bills than other customers with a

similar profile. Therefore, they could notify a client that he or she could save money by choosing a different provider. Actually, banks could even tell them which provider is cheaper. Banks could map out a family's financial situation in order to help them manage their money in a more efficient way and to make better choices. For companies, it would be perfectly possible for a bank to register their financial flows in real time and to identify difficult cash-flow situations, which would then make it easier for them to predict and manage their finances in a proactive way. It's in these types of applications that the true value of big data can be recognized.

This has also triggered new competition for banks. In France, the mobile operator Orange has started a bank. Then there is the Swedish company Klarna—it went from being a factoring company to receiving a banking license and now has an app that definitely changes how payments are done in Sweden.

New technologies also improve the accessibility of products and services that used to only be accessible to a limited circle of rich customers. Private banks are a good example of this. In the past, only rich customers could benefit from a thorough analysis of their savings and personalized advice. This actually doesn't come as a surprise, as this type of service takes a lot of work and is expensive. A private banker makes an inventory of all available financial data, conducts research into the risks, and uses this as the basis to create personal advice. Today, apps can easily collect all the information on incoming deposits, savings, investments, and clients' other financial activities. With a few algorithms and a bit of artificial intelligence, any ordinary citizen could receive quality financial advice, with a list of options corresponding to their needs and their financial situation. Multiple online banks offer this type of service.

The end
of cash

Thanks to mobile payment technology, we are moving towards a cashless society, even though we still have a long way to go. According to research by the Central European Bank, 79% of all payments are made in cash. "The results put the use of cash relative to non-cash payment methods by consumers into perspective, and indicate that the use of cash at POS is still widespread in most euro area countries. This seems to challenge the perception that cash is rapidly being replaced by cashless means of payment," is what is reported in the research.[80] Today, when small amounts of money are concerned, consumers often don't bother to use their debit card and PIN code. Most of the time, handing over a two-euro coin is faster, which partly explains why we still often use cash. But here as well things are changing, because paying with mobile technology has become much faster than using coins and bills.

Many economists support the idea of a cashless society. One of them is Geert Noels, who has said on the subject: "I find that it's a good idea, particularly because it's inevitable. Paper has become old-fashioned. Today, everything we do is digital, except what should be: making payments." However, he does identify several obstacles, distrust is definitely the most important one. "You must have a fair amount of trust in society. First of all, it must be certain that authorities won't be using these data to monitor citizens and put their savings at risk. As a society, we must also stand up to people who think that it's impossible to eradicate any form of a black economy. A cashless economy has every chance at succeeding in societies that demonstrate strong social cohesion, such as one finds in Scandinavia."[81] They use digital payment systems like Klarna, iZettle and Swish.

We must also ask ourselves what currency we would like to use to make payments with, as it's likely that we'll also be using virtual currencies. These already exist, and bitcoin is undoubtedly the most widely known. It was launched in 2009 and has become massively popular since then. Ethereum, ripple, bitcoin and litecoin are the most widely known virtual currencies—also known as crypto currencies. In early 2018, there were 1384 of them.[82] Many people have invested in them, often without truly understanding what blockchain technology really entails. Currently, bitcoin is a predominantly speculative investment, due to the many people who are hoping to get rich. Its value increase in 2017—from 900 dollars to nearly 20,000 dollars—is fascinating. This mania is similar to the internet hype in the late 90s, when companies active in the sector had no difficulty convincing people to invest. Share prices rocketed, which motivated many ordinary people to plunge into the adventure of buying their own internet shares. When the bubble burst in 2000, multiple internet companies were ruined, and those that survived built the foundations for a sector that would be better developed. We can expect a similar scenario when it comes to virtual currencies. Sooner or later, the bubble of speculations will burst, and the prices of these currencies will plummet. This will be the end for a lot of virtual currencies, but the concept of crypto currencies will remain. Other initiatives will be created after virtual currencies have failed and will bring crypto currencies to a whole new, more reliable level. It's impossible to predict what impact on the financial system, the economy, and democracy this will have, but I believe that one day, we will have a universal virtual currency instead of multiple different currencies, which will enable us to make payments all around the world, as is the case nowadays with the American dollar.

What is impressive is that multiple central banks are enabling customers to pay with virtual currencies. In 2016, the Dutch Central Bank—De Nederlandsche Bank or DNB—started with the launch of the DNBCOIN, a virtual currency the bank uses exclusively for experimenting with blockchain technology. This is a good thing. If central banks acquire a certain know-how, they can also exercise a certain amount of control over virtual currencies. This is essential in order for these currencies to acquire legitimacy as a means of payment. But we still have a very long way to go. The anonymity and simplicity of the online use of these currencies makes them a very attractive opportunity for money from criminal organizations. According to Europol, 3 to 4% of the 112 billion euros generated by crime in Europe will be laundered through the use of crypto currencies. Virtual currencies can't become an actual means of payment until they've found a way to eradicate money laundering practices and crime funding.

Banking via Facebook?

One of my children loses his debit card about every three months. We then ask the bank to block his card and send us a new one. Often, the lost card is found after a few days. But, by then, it's already too late: the old card has been permanently blocked and we have to pay to get the new one. It's not very practical. German online bank Number26 has found the solution: they've developed a system that allows their customers to temporarily block their card. If they have any doubts, a customer can block their card online. If they find it again, they can reactivate it for free. If the card hasn't surfaced after several days, customers can order a new one. It's simple, it responds to the customers' needs and it's practical.

We'll start seeing more and more of these practical applications being introduced. Banks will not be the only organizations to develop new apps and new services with the aim of facilitating the management of our finances. For several years now, the companies that develop these financial technologies have been called *fintechs*. These young companies have emerged on the market alongside traditional banks thanks to their innovative products and services. Some examples: Birdee is a robot that advises investors who are looking to invest their money online. BilltoBox is an application that digitizes invoices and allows self-employed people to process them in an easier way. MyMicroInvest allows young entrepreneurs to find funding through crowdfunding.

Fintech companies are not banks, but they're offering products and services that compete with the banks' services. This is how online companies are created. In some cases, it's easier to pay for purchases online by using PayPal, which is part of online auction marketplace eBay. PayPal isn't a bank, but an intermediary for which you need nothing but an email address. Google has introduced Google Pay, and Apple has introduced Apple Pay. These systems link customers' debit or credit card data to a smartphone or tablet, which enables them to make online purchases. All of these tech companies—big and small—have developed applications that are potentially useful, but can at the same time compete with banks.

In China, things go even further. Those who are still using a credit card are frowned upon. Paying with a card is now considered something that's just for elderly people. WeChat, the equivalent of Facebook—which currently has over a billion users—and Alipay, a subsidiary of internet company Alibaba, account for a part of all payments. The Chinese use the app to chat, transfer money, and pay their invoices. No other payment system is as "disruptive" as WeChat, and it's only a matter of time before the Chinese company's app is introduced in other countries.

Some people fear that these internet giants will become actual banks. But it's unlikely that this will happen. "A fintech can't become a bank, and vice versa. Tech companies rely on the benefits of user simplicity and speed. Banks are specialized in financial balances, risk management and they're subject to strict regulations. The latter limits opportunities. The main asset for banks lies in knowing their customers, risks, and regulations. I think that new services could be created with these assets in mind. We can compare it to a safe: in the future, banks will no longer be saving your money, but your data, which they save in a sort of digital safe," predicts Jürgen Ingels, an entrepreneur who sold his payment logistics company Clear2Pay in 2014 and has created a platform for financial-technology companies.[83]

No other sector is as heavily regulated as the banking sector. And technology companies prefer to stay away from strictly regulated environments. They're offering increasingly innovative payment services without turning into banks. Banks will be facing competition within each of their three primary fields: responsibility for payment transactions, offering savings and investment products, and loans.

Things are also unlikely to improve because, since early 2018, banks are no longer the owners of their bank transactions, as a result of the implementation of European directive PSD II (or *Payment Services Directive II*). This European regulation regulates the payment market within the European Union. The objective of these new rules is to allow third parties to have access—through your bank—to your payment data, provided of course that you have given explicit consent for this. These third parties could be a retail chain, a technology company, and even another bank. This means that you can download an app from a small technology company and let it analyze all of your payments, even when they are spread across multiple bank accounts in different banks. This could be useful, for example, for those who would like to have insight into their expenses. It's actually quite logical that the client—and not the bank—is the owner of his or her own data. This is a problem for banks because you're no longer required to use your bank's apps. It would be perfectly possible to open a bank account at a bank, but to make all your transactions with another application. The result: the bank could lose part of its relationship with its own customers, and, at the same time, this also opens the door for other banks, *fintechs* and even internet giants. This is good news for customers, who will be able to benefit from better services that will allow them to manage all of their bank accounts with just one application, including their accounts in different banks.

Is this the end of banks?

Despite the tough competition of *fintechs* and internet companies, the majority of bankers are not too worried about this. In contrast, blockchain seems to be of more concern to them. Blockchain is the technology behind the virtual currency bitcoin, among other applications. Blockchain is more advanced than all other digital technologies with which banks have been confronted until now. Previous developments have given rise to new distribution or communication channels, have made way for the emergence of new competition, or have given rise to new operational models. In contrast, blockchain can wipe out banks' justification for existence in a single blow, forcing them to completely reinvent themselves. In effect, this concerns a network that can completely decentralize financial transactions and can weaken the foundations of the current banking sector. Today, multiple intermediaries intervene in our financial transactions. Imagine that you're buying a new smartphone on the internet and you are paying with PayPal. The online payment system takes cash from you Visa account, which in turn receives the money for your purchase from your bank. These are already three intermediaries the consumer knows of. In the background, your payment goes through even more intermediaries. Moreover, every intermediary is given a small compensation as remuneration for their service, costs which affect the consumer and the web store. Hence, our payment system is not only complicated, but also very expensive, considering that every intervening party gets a little piece of the pie.

Blockchain takes all of these financial intermediaries out of the circuit. Thanks to this technology, individuals can transfer money to another individual with ease, without the intervention of a bank or other intermediary. Blockchain is a large network that looks like a long chain of boxes (hence the name "blockchain"), each containing one or multiple transactions. Furthermore, all of these blocks are connected to each other in a certain order and each block also contains information about the order of the blocks within the chain. In addition, every link in the chain receives a copy of the entire transaction chain. In other words, every party linked to the blockchain network is connected to each other and kept up to date with every move within the network. This system makes any kind of fraud impossible. Hackers who want to modify a transaction would have to modify every previous block of the transaction. They must carry out these changes multiple times, considering that every party in the network has a copy of the whole chain. This might seem very abstract, but in reality, this translates into being able to make a payment or transaction directly from one individual to another. As such, it doesn't seem so special. The power of the blockchain mainly lies in the fact that every party involved can trust each other, as the blockchain is a decentralized network of which every link monitors the transaction. This puts the banker in a different position. "Blockchain could mean the end of the 'middle men', the numerous intermediaries who have been indispensable links in our capitalist system for centuries. Whether we look at (central) banks, stock exchange clearing houses, notaries or civil status officials, they all fulfill an intermediary role that can potentially be replaced by a blockchain. [...] Not only Euroclear, but also numerous other financial institutions attempt to understand how blockchain could impact their profession and how they could react to this," is what can be read in the Flemish newspaper *De Tijd* regarding this new technology.[84]

The bank of the future

Digitalization has fundamentally changed banks. Apps have been created while branch offices have disappeared. Nearly all banks have significantly reduced their number of branches. The result: there is no longer a branch office of every large bank in your town.

"In 2016, we still saw our distribution model as a pyramid structure, with a network of branch offices at the bottom. In the coming years, this idea will change rapidly into a cylinder structure, in which digital and mobile channels have become just as important as branch offices," explains Max Jadot.[85] Bank offices won't completely disappear from the landscape, but their functions will change: offices that limit themselves to basic bank transactions have no future. These transactions can be managed directly—and more comfortably—by customers through the bank's app. In the bank of the future, everything will be about advice. Someone who needs financing for his or her company will not find their solution with an app: they have to discuss the different options with their banker. This also applies to individuals who have decided to buy a house or want to invest their savings. This added value will be the only reason for customers to go to their bank's office. But the necessity for this change is not yet clear to banks and their personnel, because this change will require a complete overhaul of the organizational structure as well as having to work outside of normal office hours. This also shows the importance of the digital evolution for the financial sector and as for every other sector it will involve the complete automation of basic services, in order to make more time and resources available for valuable advice from which customers can truly benefit.

Of course, these changes will also impact the job market. The financial sector is one of the biggest employers, but of late the number of employees has decreased significantly. In recent years, banks were quick to point the finger to digitalization in order to justify restructuring. Of course, this is partly true. At the same time, the financial crisis has forced banks to restructure, cut a large part of their services, and drastically reduce their expenses. Because of the low rates, banks have also been forced to cut their budgets. These economic factors are not related to digitalization, but are co-responsible for the loss of jobs in the financial sector. However, banks continue to recruit new staff, but in the digital era, they're looking for people with different skill profiles. They need fewer administrative employees and more people who are skilled in informatics and more advisors.

Your insurer is watching out for burglars

In recent years, banks have been the subject of thorough reor-
ganizations, so they can adapt more quickly, even when they are
not yet completely equipped to face Chinese internet companies such as WeChat and Alibaba. In contrast, insurance companies are lagging behind. Unlike banks, these companies have
not been forced to reinvent themselves after the financial crisis
and have continued to function as if the world had not changed
at all. The result: banks have amazing apps available, while we
are still waiting for the first proper app from the insurance industry. How can this be explained? Insurance companies are
facing two fundamental problems. On the one hand, they're
dealing with a negative image, as was confirmed by a survey carried out by GFK during the second half of 2017, given to 1130 individuals and 151 self-employed people, regarding their experiences with insurance and insurers. What can we conclude?
Nearly 57% believe that their insurer doesn't listen to them
when they're not happy. A mere 23% find insurance products
easy to understand, and seven out of ten individuals think that
they have to read and sign far too many documents in order to
take out a new contract. Furthermore, 25% of all insured people
who said they were satisfied with a recent insurance settlement
are not certain whether things will go just as well next time. So,
distrust seems to be a major factor.[86] The second problem is that
insurance companies only contact their customers when there's
a problem. And those clients who haven't made a claim are only
contacted by their insurer when it's time to pay the bill. The
situation is different for banks, because consumers use their
products on a daily basis.

In a digital world, insurers are running the risk of finding themselves in a very vulnerable position. Digital consumers have very high expectations, particularly in terms of service quality, that should be commensurate with the substantial sums of money they spend on insurance every year. This is what consumers benefit from in other sectors today. So insurance companies need to completely redefine their role: instead of limiting their customer contact to moments when there is a problem, they have to become systems whose biggest concern at all times is their customers' wellbeing. Insurers have to think bigger. Consumers will certainly appreciate it if their insurer gives them advice; for example, by communicating to them what the best smoke detectors are when they purchase a fire insurance policy. Another example: regarding protection against theft, your insurer could inform you about the existence of applications with which you can check if your home is secure from a distance. This way, insurers could take on a new role, which would definitely be appreciated by consumers. This modern insurer will become—figuratively speaking, of course—a kind of caretaker who helps you avoid certain problems and who doesn't just show up when things go wrong. Insurers will not only be able to insure you, but at the same time, they'll be able to ensure your security and your health. A lot of people would undoubtedly be willing to pay for these services in the form of a subscription.

We are slowly—but certainly—moving in this direction. Several insurers have already introduced apps that warn their client in case of storms, snow, or hail, which enables them to take the necessary measures to reduce damage. Also, for cars, there are multiple digital solutions. For example, since early 2017, it has been possible to signal a collision via your smartphone. With the QR-code of their insurance document, car drivers can send the information about the accident from the accident location itself. Then, all you have to do is enter information regarding the circumstances of the accident and fill out the claim form, including adding pictures. It's practical, but it's nothing more than a simple digitization of an existing service. The applications of certain insurers are more innovative, in the sense that they analyze their customers' behavior while driving and give them advice for a safer and cheaper driving style. These applications are far from revolutionary, but they do show that insurance companies are moving in the right direction. Nevertheless, they could be moving faster. These new services will be launched on the market. The question is who will develop the best services for the inhabitants of Digitalis: the insurers or technology companies?

CHAPTER 10

The media is everywhere

How can the media
reinvent itself?

In 1995, I was the chief executive of a large industrial laundry.
There, I experienced something that would change my professional career completely: for the first time, I had to communicate with American shareholders electronically. Back then,
this process was still very complicated, and I sent my very first
email. In that moment, I felt the winds of change. I had an interesting position in an international company. I had a good
salary and a company car. But, I sensed that something was
coming, that the future was taking on a different shape. And
I definitely didn't want to miss out on this opportunity. Less
than a year later, I joined the innovation subsidiary of VUM,
editor of, among other things, the Flemish newspapers
De Standaard and *Het Nieuwsblad*, where I devoted myself to internet projects. *De Standaard* was about to launch its website
and wanted to evolve. However, it was difficult to convince the
parent company to take on the digital adventure any sooner. In
1996, we had, nevertheless, succeeded in launching Clickx, a
kind of (printed!) "TV magazine" about the internet. Back then,
there were no more than 300,000 Belgian internet users, who
knew hardly anything about it. The web progressively made its

way to media, and in the late 90s, things had changed completely: the internet had become a true hype. I helped to shape the Belgian media from the front lines in a key moment; and this process is still ongoing.

News topics and the need for information are ever-present in today's society. In the past, we read our newspaper in the morning and watched the news on TV in

The ways in which news is published are changing, but the demand remains unaltered.

the evening. We received information twice a day. Today, we use media in a completely different way: in fact, we "consume" it throughout the entire day. We regularly check sites for information or the stream of information on social media. All the news that reaches us during our downtime isn't necessarily interesting, and we often consume it "like a snack". That does not prevent us from spending more time on media than ever before. This clearly contradicts the views of people who have tried to predict the future in the past, namely that digitalization would mean the end of traditional media. This fear is understandable because the introduction of new media has always led to much concern. When the printing press was developed, people feared that the human brain would not be capable of absorbing so much information. In the 16th century, some people had similar objections regarding notebooks as a memory aid, and a century later, people had the same attitude towards cafés, popular places for exchanging news.[87] It's a familiar tale. Nevertheless, throughout the centuries, new forms of media kept being created, such as newspapers, radio, television and (mobile) internet. Human beings haven't drowned in the flood of information and different forms of media, which have become an integral part of our daily lives.

The ways in which news is published are changing, but the demand remains unaltered.

Paying
for information

Print media was one of the first to understand how the internet could change the industry. Audiovisual media remained unaffected for a long time because the use of videos was difficult and slow at the beginning of the internet era. Computers and their internet connections were not functioning smoothly enough. The video platform YouTube didn't exist until 2005. For newspapers and magazines, things were different.

When the internet first started, websites contained mostly text and pictures. So, this was exactly the same content as newspapers and magazines had, which forced them to digitalize their information early on. During the 90s, not only were you able to find information by reading the paper edition of newspapers, but also by going to their websites. The benefit of digitalization was that information was dematerialized. Newspapers no longer depended exclusively on paper newspaper sales for distributing their articles. Digitalization has widened their potential public significantly. Journalists no longer only write for newspaper readers, but also for people who visit their (mobile) website or digital newspaper. Between July 2015 and July 2016, an average of 1.2 million paper and digital newspapers were sold every day in Belgium. The sales of newspapers has decreased to a lesser extent than was expected, partly thanks to digitalization.

At the same time, the number of visitors of newspaper websites has increased to an average of 4.9 million visitors every day, and this number does not include mobile apps, which means that the number of readers is probably much higher.[88] Newspaper publishers are certainly selling fewer paper newspapers, but they've never had more readers. Surely, this is bad news for publishers who think of themselves as sellers of paper newspapers, but it's an advantage for those who are committed to providing as many people as possible with quality journalism.

Paper newspapers are comparable to the candle market. Two centuries ago, candles were essential for providing light. Those who thought that candles would remain the best source of light turned out to be wrong. But those who thought candles would become obsolete were also wrong. Scented and luxury candles are a successful business in today's society, as is proven by the success of Baobab. I think that paper newspapers will become a luxury product, while digital versions will reach a larger public.

Increasing your public is one thing, but being profitable is a different story. In the past, it was simple: publishers made money by selling newspapers and magazines. Furthermore, they increased their number of readers by advertising: the more readers a medium has, they more expensive advertising in the newspaper or magazine was. That's how it was until the 90s. The internet changed everything. Soon, newspapers had more free readers than paying ones because a large part of the public paid absolutely nothing in order to access news articles online. Furthermore, newspapers quickly realized that the income from online advertisements was nowhere near what advertisers were willing to pay for paper newspapers. Newspaper publishers were faced with the challenge of making money while having readers who—at the beginning at least—paid nothing. This seems to be a paradox, but is definitely not impossible to manage.

The new business model departs from the idea of free online news that's available for everybody. At this point, publishers don't have high incomes. Online advertising revenues equal just a few cents for every website visitor. But, people who surf the website and consume free information will sooner or later stumble upon paid articles. If they're convinced that the information is high quality, a portion of the internet visitors will be willing to pay for a digital subscription. This could be the first step towards another subscription, such as a paper version of the weekend edition, for example, which will be delivered to your house every Saturday morning. This way, newspapers can progressively turn free news article readers into subscribers. But, it doesn't end here. Those who are true fans of a newspaper might be tempted to make purchases in the online store of their favorite media website. Today, newspaper web stores sell all kinds of products: books about wine, in addition to LED lights and solar panels. The result: every website visit is a potential source of income, even when the visitor initially only consumes free information. This business model is nothing new: it's the same one as that of Silicon Valley, which has enabled large internet companies to build their empires. There is even a word for this model (created by consultant FaberNovel): *GAFA-economics*, in which GAFA is an acronym for Google, Amazon, Facebook and Apple. Currently, these companies generate annual sales revenues of several billions of dollars with services that are completely free. Facebook is free and has over two billion users at the moment. Every day, several billions of key words are added to Google's search engine. These companies are not making any money from this, but they are mobilizing billions of users, who are the starting point of many paid services and advertisements.

Some were certain that these new business models would mean the end of quality journalism, but thus far, this hasn't proved to be the case, and I'm confident that the media has the ability to reinvent itself. However, journalism will not be able to avoid having to search for new financial models. Newspaper publishers remain profitable today, but they're struggling.

"The main challenge always lies ahead. With digitalization, media corporations are reaching an increasing number of readers, but that doesn't mean that they are more profitable, on the contrary. The biggest challenge concerns the advertising market, due to radical changes that are about to happen," writes Christian Van Thillo, CEO of De Persgroep, one of the biggest media corporations in Europe, in the group's 2016 annual report.[89] "For years, we had been part of a game, of which we had mastered every facet and all the rules were clear. Today, the game has changed, with other players and other rules that are constantly changing. We have to find a business model that will be capable of ensuring our success in the long term."

Google is trying to contribute to the future of publishers and, in 2016, it introduced the Digital News Initiative, an exchange program for publishers, with the aim of stimulating innovation. This project has given rise to multiple new products and initiatives. There is also a fund of 150 million dollars available to help finance innovative digital projects in the media sector.

A television screen for everyone

The world of television is facing digital challenges similar to those of the written press, but broadcasting companies are not yet as advanced when it comes to digitalization. This delay can be explained by the fact that the audiovisual market is a very structured market, where public authorities still play an important role. Authorities continue to play a leading role in the television sector, simply because making television is very expensive. This was particularly the case when television first started; television studios were so expensive that public authorities were the only ones that could afford them. The written press was forced to change its strategy from the very beginning of the digital era, by having to create new business models and continuously refining them. Broadcasting companies observed these changes from a distance and continued making television the same way they had always done. Suddenly, things started changing very quickly, and companies were forced to deal with reality: television viewers were watching significantly less "linear" television (in real time), which had been the case since the very first TV broadcasts. Daily television use had even decreased among elderly viewers. The smartphone is now in second place. Nearly 31% of all smartphone users watch videos on their mobile phone every day. Additionally, among young people, smartphones seem to have taken the place of televisions, with 69% of young people aged between 15 and 19 watching videos on their smartphone every day, versus 54% who watch television every day.[90]

The digitalization of TV programs has enabled television viewers to skip advertisements, which is of course problematic for a sector that lives off of those revenues. Furthermore, television viewers no longer follow a TV schedule. Watching a TV program at a different time has become the norm. In addition, conventional channels have to compete with a medium they hadn't expected to enter this market: the internet. YouTube is a video platform that is much more popular than conventional television (particularly among young people), and an increasing number of people subscribe to streaming services, such as Netflix, for watching the latest series, and all without advertisements! In the meantime, cable operators are also starting to create their own content.

But people haven't decided to stop watching television because conventional "linear" TV is about to disappear. Many families find themselves sitting together in front of the TV without anyone actually watching. Everyone is looking at their smartphone or tablet, and everybody is constantly talking about what they are watching. The big screen isn't disappearing, but a different way of using other screens is emerging. Watching television will become interactive, which will bring people together in a new way.

Despite all these challenges, TV channels and producers have one huge advantage: in our new digital world, videos have become the preferred mode of communication, which happens to be their specialty. Never before have people watched so many videos. On YouTube alone, 400 hours of new videos are added every minute. In just a few days, more content is uploaded to the platform than all of the content generated by public television corporations over the last ten years combined. And the majority of all users watch videos on a mobile device. This no longer comes as a surprise, because everybody has seen people in the train or in the park watching videos on their smartphones. When the smartphone was introduced, nobody could have imagined that this device would be used to watch movies. In fact, videos have become a new form of communication. Until the end of the 19th century, people communicated solely in written form. Then came pictures, and today technology allows us to add videos. Additionally, digitalization has made the world of video more democratic. Until recently, only big players in the world of media were able to make audiovisual content. They were actually the only ones capable of buying the required equipment for it. Today, any young person can produce a short film and distribute it, without any difficulty.

Bye bye
to radio?

The first thing my children do when they step into the car is switch off the radio and listen to the music on their smartphones, via the streaming service Spotify, for example. This doesn't bode well for the future of radio stations that are not yet very advanced in terms of digitalization.

For radio stations, it's not only about the way in which they broadcast, but also the actual foundation of radio. There is little chance that young people will continue to listen to radio stations, especially when radio programs contain advertisements. An increasing number of people are creating their music playlists on the basis of the almost infinite number of songs that streaming services have to offer. This development will continue without end, particularly because all cars will be connected to the internet. Therefore, it's certain that the number of radio station listeners will continue to decrease in the future.

Just like other forms of media, radio stations are forced to reinvent themselves. They are actually very aware of this. The producer of radio Nostalgie, Nathalie Schoonbaert, told Flemish newspaper *De Tijd*: "The digital evolution will simply mean the end of radio if we idly stand by. [...] For me, the unique selling point of radio lies in the essential nature of it. Radio creates a unique environment that is about more than just listening to music. Every channel has its own way of presenting its programs and, by doing so, is building its own community. That's why radio must have more contact with listeners. In addition to the presenter, it's important to interact by telephone and through social media, in order to stimulate discussions. An interesting interview can take on a life of its own on the web with an article on our website or on Facebook. Radio must develop from a one-way form of communication to an interactive one. Otherwise we will lose the new generation, who also really like expressing themselves."[91]

It's likely that a significant number of functions of radio as we know it today will become obsolete. Take weather forecasts and traffic information: we are much more inclined to check our smartphones than to listen to the radio.

Despite everything, radio still has interesting aspects. Audio communication is more relevant than ever before. Take intelligent speakers, for example, which you can control with your voice and that can also provide spoken information. Users of Google Home often ask it to listen to the news. That is why Google's engineers have experimented with different options in order to respond to this demand, and have conducted research in to what users consider the best way to listen to news through their speakers. The result? Spoken news broadcasts are still the best way to respond to their needs. Listening to newspaper articles takes too long and is not dynamic enough, except for specific news topics, such as the winner of a country's elections or the score of the last Real Madrid match.

Social media, Digitalis' "town square"

Digitalization has also given rise to a new form of media: social media. These are platforms where everyone can share their messages, knowledge or experiences. In the world of media, it's a true revolution, because it's the users who are defining the content of the media. We use Facebook to share messages or short videos with friends. On LinkedIn, we can build a professional network with the aim of advancing our careers, and with

Twitter we can share our opinion on pretty much every subject with the rest of the world.

Compared to other forms of media, social media are still in the early stages. The first platform was the American network Classmates.com. Created in 1995, it allowed users to find old classmates or colleagues that they had lost contact with. In 1997, we witnessed the launch of SixDegrees.com, which already had more in common with the social networking sites we know today. The name of the internet website comes from the theory that every person in the world is connected through a maximum of six contacts and that we are all connected to each other through the friends of our friends and colleagues of our colleagues. The real social media breakthrough took place in 2003, with the creation of the American company MySpace, which became the largest online social network in the world. Users could publish mostly pictures, videos, music and blogs. MySpace made it possible for the rock band Arctic Monkeys and the singer Lily Allen, among others, to become famous. The creation of Facebook in 2006 meant the end of MySpace. In 2010, Facebook already had half a million active users and it passed the 2 billion mark in 2017.[92]

Today, it's difficult to imagine a world without social media. Nearly 85% of all internet users have a social media account. On average, they spend about one and a half hours a day using it.[93] Social networks have become the ideal meeting place in Digitalis: you can meet friends for a nice conversation or you can get in touch with old friends. It can be a tool for increasing social cohesion in a country with over 4 billion inhabitants. At the same time, it's a relatively new form of media, and we still have to learn how to use it in our daily lives, just like we had to do when newspapers, radio and television first appeared.

Social media has also confronted us with a dilemma: on the one hand, users are willing to share very personal information on the internet, but on the other hand, they're afraid that their right to privacy is at risk. We'll discuss this problem in further detail in the following chapter. On another note, several studies indicate that using social media intensively increases the risk of depression.[94] When they look at other people's beautiful pictures and "status updates", some people can be led to think that those people are happier. Cyber bullying and internet addiction can make the situation even worse. But, at the moment, nobody has been able to demonstrate that social media and depression are actually connected. Because it might also be that people who are susceptible to depression use social media more frequently in order to make themselves feel more complete.

One other problem caused by social media is the phenomenon of fake news, or in other words, the distribution of false information intended to influence the public opinion. Social media platforms are involved in the distribution of fake news.

Social networks have become the ideal meeting place in Digitalis: you can meet friends for a nice conversation or you can get in touch with old friends.

Contrary to traditional media, the platform content is not being checked. This is the users' own responsibility. But, on a platform with dozens of millions, possibly billions, of users who can share anything with one click, false information is being circulated at the speed of light. The result: the pressure on social media websites increases. They are being asked—rightly so—to treat the information shared with the rest of the world on their platform with more caution. Fake news is a potential time bomb for democracy, as it allows for populist ideas to be spread around the world and influence citizens who might be making important decisions on the basis of false information. From now on, we must ask ourselves what the impact of fake news has been on the American elections, and on the result of the Brexit referendum in Great Britain, where false news was being circulated, particularly in the all-powerful tabloid newspapers, who have been against the European Union for many years.

So, fake news is not a new phenomenon. For conventional journalists, this situation creates opportunities, as citizens are in need of explanations and context more than ever before. We're living in a world that is becoming increasingly complex, and investigative journalists represent an important weapon against fake news. It can certainly be tempting to read the same articles continuously or to publish the same stories without checking them all carefully. At the same time, mobile technologies and social media are forcing journalists to distribute their messages in a highly summarized format, at the expense of fact checking. It poses a great challenge and a real problem for journalists.

Furthermore, the amount of available media keeps increasing, as digital channels make it much easier to publish information. Today, everyone can become a journalist or producer by using their own internet website, Facebook page, or YouTube channel, and go looking for people who are interested. The availability of media has never before been so vast. "The challenge conventional forms of media are facing consists of withstanding the tough competition. Particularly, by competing on equal terms and therefore using the possibilities that digital communication channels have to offer in a creative way. Another way of competing consists of offering added value, by using expertise and journalistic experience that is available in-house. And, by continuing to respect ethical rules of journalism. The quality of information is the most important asset traditional media has to compete with the new challengers," was stated in a published analysis by Flemish newspaper *De Tijd*.[95]

In early 2018, readers of the French-language newspaper *Le Soir* chose the word "fake news" as the most important new word of the year. It was a worrying development, in their opinion. In an interview with the newspaper, Martine Simonis argued for journalism to demand quality as a "brand". According to her, this strategy "will be in a better position to fight misinformation than coercive legal measures that are not very suitable for social media, where there are no limits." This was an indirect response to French President Macron's recent push to enact legislation against misinformation online, stated the newspaper.

An ordinary day in 2028

Innovations are developing at an increasingly faster pace and on a global scale. The result: it has become extremely difficult to design projects or make plans that extend beyond a year. It's practically impossible to predict what the world of media will look like in 2028. However, this was the question I was asked by the Flemish media minister, Sven Gatz, in 2016 for his book *Over media heb ik niets te zeggen* (I have nothing to say about media). This was an interesting question to answer, which I would gladly share here (with some alterations). What we know for certain is that everyone will always be connected to the internet or something that will replace the internet. This will no longer require impractical keyboards or large smartphones, but will be connected via a single, intelligent environment. What will an ordinary day be like ten years from now?

> In the morning, I get ready to have breakfast. The most recent information is projected on the (white) tabletop.

Not any information, but "my" information: customized to my preferences and my ongoing need for news topics, with some news topics that I wouldn't choose myself and that have been suggested by journalists that I have selected in order to expand my horizons. This service is brought to me by MediaValley, which automatically charges me for the articles I read or consult via micro payments. I receive a mixture of texts, pictures and videos. The table is re-filled, I watch, I move around several texts and images, I look more closely at some of them and I leave a few others to watch later on. My digital agenda alerts me via that same table-screen that it's time to leave the house. I get into the driverless car that comes to pick me up. I can consult information that I just selected on the windshield. I ask for more details, and I watch several 3D videos. There is no radio in the car. This type of media, an established favorite of commuters, has simply disappeared.

Barely half an hour later, I arrive at the office and I start with a management meeting. Six colleagues are standing around a high table together. Relevant news and company results are projected on the table-screen. Here as well, the professional news topics are provided by MediaValley. The more personalized the information is, the more expensive it is. In fact, there's not a single minute that I'm not connected to media products offered by MediaValley or its competitors: always the right information, at the right moment, always relevant, entertaining or useful. These companies distribute news articles, both in our country and in the rest of the world. There are very few foreign correspondents. National news, developed by local journalists who are familiar with the context, is distributed across the globe.

In the evening, my children and I watch a game show on TV that's still popular, called *Numbers and Letters*. In the meantime, over a hundred countries have bought the concept and have created one in their own language. Every family member has his or her own screen, projected onto the coffee table, where each can decipher the answers. We can compare our own results and those of other television viewers who are watching the broadcast at the same time. Lively discussions take place. The experience has more in common with a board game than with a conventional television game show, just as it was ten years ago. We also get ready for "71", an animated game by Jean Michel Zecca on RTL, that tests us on general knowledge and in which you can directly participate online. We challenge ourselves in a playful way, competing with local officials and other stars invited onto the show. Then, we decide to watch the latest episode of a national crime show. This show is so successful that it can be watched all over the world. The episodes are short and last half an hour and we watch four of them. PrixNet charges us for every episode we watch. For those who create media and art, the domestic market is nothing more than a stepping stone to the international stage, which is where the majority of their revenue is generated.

This may all seem like a fantasy, but in reality, this is most likely what the future will hold. The technology necessary to create everything I just described already exists, as does the creativity, the demand for local content, quality information and familiar celebrities. This scenario also shows that the future of Digitalis isn't just something that's going to happen in the future, it's already started today.[96]

CHAPTER 11

Trust in Digitalis

What about personal data
protection and online safety?

When Google launched Google Street View in Belgium in 2011, a feature that provides panoramic views from positions along many streets in the world, it caused a major uproar. I even received a telephone call on my home phone from a clearly irritated person who found it completely unacceptable that people were able to see the facade of his house on the internet. I calmly explained to him that we could blur his house, so that it couldn't be identified on the web. And I also asked him, between the two of us, who was the biggest victim of a breach of privacy here: him, because his house could be seen on the internet, as it could be seen by anyone who passed the house on the street, or me, bothered by a telephone call on my private number when I wanted to spend time with my children, just to hear his complaints? This question calmed him down.

People often ask for their property to be made unrecognizable on Google Street View. These same people then contact Google to ask them to make it visible again, because they've changed their minds, because they want to sell their house, or because they find that they reacted too impulsively. They are then surprised to hear that Google cannot carry out their request, as the images have been permanently erased, as have the back-ups. This illustrates two things: first of all, that the discussion surrounding the right to privacy is also influenced by people's emotions, and secondly, that companies sometimes go further than people think in order to protect personal data.

In Digitalis, the right to privacy is a bigger priority than ever before. Online stores know which product you'll like best, banks advise you to switch to a cheaper energy provider, doctors analyze your symptoms by using artificial intelligence, the GPS app on your smartphone helps you to avoid traffic jams, supermarkets take money directly from your bank account when you shop for groceries, all the way to your refrigerator that tells you when you're running out of milk... All these applications are not only very practical, but already technically possible at this very moment. But none of these applications can function without the user's data. These data have always been available, but never in such significant quantities. According to the IDC research agency, the digital world is expected to increase to the size of 180 Zettabytes by 2025, which is the number 180 followed by 21 zeros.[97] In 2016, there were already more devices connected to the internet than there are people in the world. According to these sources, the number of devices connected to the internet is expected to increase to 20, to 100 billion in the future, which will mean an explosive increase in data. A large part of these data are personal data, or in other words, the digital traces you leave behind with every click or change on your screen.

Therefore, it's no coincidence that the protection of personal data has become one of the main questions of the digital revolution. On the one hand, we've never given away as much information about ourselves on social media as we do now (in the past, it would have been unthinkable to share pictures of your children with several hundreds of "friends"), and today, a surprising number of us have no problem with this. We're also willing to exchange personal data with companies in exchange for free services or privileges. But on the other hand, we're more worried about what will happen with our data and how companies or governments use them. So, we have to look for a good balance: good quality services and innovation can go hand in hand with the right to privacy.

The fear
of Big Brother

These worries related to the right to privacy are not a recent development. The concept comes from the United States, where two lawyers wrote an article in the legal journal *Harvard Law Review*, entitled *The Right to Privacy*, in 1890. It was a reaction to the rise of new printing technologies, which was the foundation of a new media industry. Newspapers, now widely available, contain pictures and at times revealing information about famous celebrities. This was unheard of at the time. At the same time, society had undergone fundamental changes: the industrialization and urbanization characteristic of the 19th century had given rise to a certain degree of anonymity.[98] Tensions arose between the new forms of media and the private sphere.

The right to privacy appeared in 1948 in Article 8 of the Universal Declaration of Human Rights. When it comes to privacy, we often refer to it as the "right to privacy". On the website of the Belgian Ministry of Justice, it's stated that "every person has the right to privacy and family life, except for the cases and conditions established by law (Belgian Constitution, Article 22)". Europe goes even further by also considering a person's home and correspondence as private. The right to privacy also includes "respect for personal data", which means "the protection of personal data, the right to not provide personal information and to only share data that is strictly necessary, the right to know what personal data is being saved by third parties, the way in which they are collected and used". This concept, which has been developed in recent years, has become the subject of growing concerns. And rightly so.

Just 25 years ago, the right to privacy only applied to publications that we received in our mailboxes, unsolicited phone calls and, increasingly, advertising emails that we received in our inboxes. But the development of the internet has undeniably created new tensions. Today, everybody can publish messages on the internet that can be seen by thousands, or even millions of people. Everyone with a smartphone always has a camera available with which they can film people and upload the video to Facebook and Twitter in the blink of an eye. In a few clicks, employers can find tons of personal information about job candidates, because the internet registers everything you do online. So it will come as no surprise that the concept of the right to privacy has evolved. Today, many people are concerned about the information that is being circulated about them in the digital world, and how it might be used.

What is telling is that, in early 2017, George Orwell's science fiction novel *1984* made it onto Amazon's bestseller list in the United States.[99] Even though the novel was published in 1949, it's an incredibly relevant book today. In the book, Orwell wrote about a totalitarian state, where the party leader of the "superstate" Oceania—Big Brother—decides how people ought to behave and has permanent control over their actions, even in people's homes, through the use of cameras. The famous slogan *"Big Brother is watching you"* is becoming increasingly relevant in today's society.

The importance
of the right to privacy

Companies are not allowed to use customers' and users' data for just any reason. Data are also being called "the new gold" or "the new oil", because we're talking about a type of raw material that can be sold and with which you can make money. But exactly the opposite is true. This is what Dutch bank ING found out—at its own expense. In 2014, one of the bank's directors opened a Pandora's box during an interview with Dutch economic newspaper *Het Financieele Dagblad*, in which he said that the bank wanted to conduct an experiment with big data, with the help of its customers. For this project, data regarding customers and their transactions would be used for personalized advertisements from other companies. For instance, a client of ING who spends a significant amount of money on garden supplies every spring would receive special offers from garden centers. This project caused such outrage that numerous customers went so far as to consider leaving the bank. ING tried to convince them to stay by assuring them that the data of their customers would never leave the bank. But the damage was already done, because everybody was convinced that their data would be sold. A little while later, the project was discontinued entirely, for a good reason. Client data are not raw material that companies can sell. They are a means of getting to know their customers better, so that they can offer them better services or develop new products. In fact, many websites analyze visitors' behavior in order to provide them with targeted advertisements. But displaying an advertisement on a screen is very different from selling data. Advertisers don't know who receives their advertisements. Furthermore, internet users have to click on the advertisement before they enter the advertiser's website. Also, internet users can easily modify the settings of their internet browser in order to block or filter advertisements. This can also be done through the privacy settings of your Google account, which enables users to have control over their data and to indicate that they no longer want to receive targeted advertisements. Moreover, Google tries to display relevant advertisements that are non-invasive and short enough so that internet users can easily ignore them if they're not interested.

Data could create opportunities for more ease of use or a better shopping experience. New consumers often have no problem with having to share some personal data, on the condition that it's useful: on the basis of geo-localization data, Waze can offer consumers a GPS app. With all your payment data in your bank's application, you can track your expenses in more detail, and on the basis of your online behavior, *Le Monde* can suggest newspaper articles that might be of interest to you. The most important condition for sharing personal data is of course that you're going to get something for it in return.

A second condition is that you give your permission. This doesn't mean that websites have to ask for your permission for every single action. Take cookies, for example. These are files that websites place on your computer, so that they will recognize you when you visit the website again. Cookies enable you to view the website in your preferred language or memorize your internet settings. In practice, it's impossible for every website to ask you for your permission to use cookies over and over again, the user experience would suffer. First and foremost, users must know what the permission is for and it must be asked for in a transparent and comprehensible way. I don't feel comfortable when I have to give permission for access to my list of contacts, pictures, geo-localization data and my camera when installing a new app. All these options are often necessary for the application to function properly, but most of the time, we aren't using them all at the same time. I think that it would make much more sense and be more acceptable if applications asked for your permission when it's truly necessary. For example, the app might ask you for access to your camera right when you want to take a picture, and for access to your pictures, on the condition that you agree to share them. This is the only way in which we can have control over things. Besides, maybe you do not want the creator of a certain app to record the place where you are, banks to collect your payment data, or newspapers to register the articles you read. You must be able to refuse such permissions. The result is that you might not have access to certain services or applications, but that is a personal choice.

Data protection technology

Companies are not only supposed to be capable of ensuring the correct treatment of your data, but they also have to show that they're doing everything in their power to protect it. Companies might have strict policies regarding the right to privacy, but this isn't much use if customers' data are not protected and are available to people with bad intentions. This is one of the biggest challenges the modern world is facing.

Today, hacking is no longer an exception to the rule. In November 2018, 500 million customers of the Marriott Hotel Chain were victims of Chinese Hackers. And in 2017, over 200,000 computers were infected by the WannaCry virus. Then, the hackers asked for a "ransom", which victims had to pay before they could access their computers again. According to Europol, the European agency specialized in fighting crime;

this unprecedented attack was mainly aimed at companies. And these are merely a few examples among many.

Hacking weakens public trust in digitalization. That is why companies must do everything in their power to protect their data and those of their customers. The way in which Google protects its data centers says much about this challenge. I'll begin with the physical protection of websites, which is like a fortress, under permanent protection. Also, there is cyber security. Data are encrypted with the use of the most recent techniques. Furthermore, the data of any single individual are distributed to multiple servers in different data centers. Even if hackers happen to succeed in stealing the data, they would be unusable and illegible, and the hackers could never have all the data of one user.

The fight against hacking is a constant fight; it requires a great deal of knowledge and big investments. For small companies, it's often impossible or unaffordable to put such a system in place. The best solution for these SMEs is to save their information in the cloud, rather than on their own servers. Large companies such as Microsoft, Amazon, IBM, the French company OVH, or Google offer these types of cloud solutions and have the means and expertise necessary to keep their security systems up to date.

The importance of a strong password

Companies are obliged to secure their data and those of their customers, but we are also responsible for protecting our own data. Too often, users themselves are the weakest link when it comes to data protection. A company specialized in computer security, Symantec, thinks that cybercriminals have already stolen 146 billion euros from 978 million victims in 2017. It often involves identity theft, credit card fraud or password thefts. "Globally, cybercrime victims share a similar profile. They are almost twice as likely to own a connected home device as non-victims, but have blind spots when it comes to cyber security basics. For example, cybercrime victims tend to use the same password across all online accounts, diminishing the value of using a secure password," explains Symantec.[100] Furthermore, many have given at least one password to a third party and their passwords are often very "weak". Security company SplashData reviews the most frequently used passwords every year, these are also the easiest for hackers to crack. In recent years, the most frequently used password was "123456" followed by "password" and "12345678"![101] Personal passwords, such as the names or birthdates of your children can be easily found by hackers, because much of this information is available on social media. Real protection means having a different, long, and complex password for every single account belonging to an individual user.

In 2012, the Belgian banking sector federation, Febelfin, stirred things up by publishing a short educational film in which the main role was played by Dave, a fortune teller. A white tent was installed in the middle of Brussels. Pedestrians were invited to come and meet Dave. They were told that Dave could read their thoughts and that the session would be filmed for a television show. The participants were amazed when they heard what Dave knew about them. For example, he knew what the color of their motorcycle was, the name of their best friend, or the number of boyfriends/girlfriends they had had. He was able to describe their house, knew their bank account number, how much money they had, and how much they spent on clothes. At the end of the meeting, the participants found out that a team of hackers, hidden behind a curtain, had looked up all the information about them. The message *"Your entire life is online"* was displayed on a screen. The participants were surprised to see how much information about them was available on the web.[102]

"In order to develop, the digital economy needs trust and security. Ending certain illegal practices won't be enough. Users must also know what they should and should not do in order to protect themselves. Everyone knows that they should always lock the door of their house, but a good number of citizens don't know how to secure their online data," said Alexander De Croo, the Belgian Deputy Prime Minister, after the launch of educational website cypersimple.be.[103] This website is the result of a close collaboration between consumer association Test-Achats, the Belgian government, and Google. The goal is to encourage citizens to strengthen their online protection. The internet is an amazing tool that enables great discoveries, along with opportunities to create and to collaborate. But, in order to use it in the best way possible, it's important to ensure safety.

The right to privacy is more important than ever before. Of course we must do everything we can to keep our society from turning into a Big Brother society. European regulation GDPR (*General Data Protection Regulation*) is, in any event, a legal tool that aims to provide for more clarity and harmony within this field.

We're moving towards a society in which cameras are omnipresent. These cameras are particularly useful for enhancing security. Their presence discourages many criminals. Furthermore, certain cameras are also equipped with a facial recognition system.[104] This can be very useful, for example using facial recognition technology to search for stalkers at concerts.[105]

Does this scare you? In that case, think about the Internet of Things, which will register all your interactions with devices that are installed in your home, and that will bring "surveillance" to a whole new level, because you'll be using intelligent speakers and cameras throughout your entire house. These will, of course, be connected to the internet, which will create a both many advantages and many disadvantages. In recent years, it has appeared that devices that are part of the Internet of Things were easy targets for people with bad intentions. In 2015, two computer hackers showed American technology magazine *Wired* how they could take control of a Jeep Cherokee from a distance. They were able to stop the car, turn on the windshield wipers, the radio and the air conditioning. In the end, the manufacturer had to recall 1.4 million cars. A year later, nearly 80 security cameras manufactured by Sony were revealed to contain faults, which enabled cybercriminals to access people's photographs. In 2017, a "leak" was discovered in a robotic vacuum cleaner by LG. A hacker had been able to take control of the small camera installed in the device and other intelligent devices by LG, such as refrigerators and air conditioning systems. That same year, it was found that toy manufacturer Spiral Toys had clearly not been able to secure its talking teddy bears, to which parents could connect their smartphones, so they could talk to their children from a distance. Millions of conversations were wiretapped.[106]

We are living in a completely new world, which offers lots of opportunities, but presents dangers as well. We must face this together, so that we can continue to benefit from the incredible advantages these new technologies have to offer.

Is this a reason to prevent the technological evolution? No, of course not. People will continue to buy these kinds of devices.

However, they must be secured. Safety and the protection of the right to privacy are important for everybody: (internet) companies, public authorities and citizens. We are living in a completely new world, which offers lots of opportunities, but some dangers as well. We must face this together, so that we can continue to benefit from the incredible advantages these new technologies have to offer. Let's make Digitalis a safe country.

Part 3 _____ Reinventing Europe

CHAPTER 12

The past shows us the way to the future

We might have forgotten it, but in the past, we've reinvented ourselves multiple times and Europe was at the center of the international scene. Not that things were so much better then, as some older generations wrongly claim. Over the past centuries and years, we've certainly made progress. But we have lost our ambitions and dreams. However, this is exactly what we need to do today: dare to dream. Why shouldn't we be able to rekindle our passions? A fish will grow as much as its bowl allows. Just like children need space to grow, workers must have the opportunity to blossom, and independent entrepreneurs and companies won't develop when they are discouraged from doing so.

In European countries, the bowl—which defines the limits of the dreams of our politicians and business leaders—is much too small. Why do European technology and biotechnology companies often prefer to be taken over by a foreign shareholder as soon as they are big enough to go international?

We need investors who look 30 years into the future instead of just three or five years. We also need legal security and a transparent fiscal system that doesn't continually change, time and time again. And I'm not even talking about the need to develop good mobility and to offer quality education.

But the main success factor is ambition. We have plenty of money, but we must be willing to create worldwide players. The whole of Europe would benefit from this: it would stimulate the job market, which increases the available means for R&D in the knowledge economy, so other companies can benefit from it in turn.

Companies are like gold- *The main success factor*
fish: they adapt to their envi- *is ambition.*
ronment. In a pond, goldfish
have sufficient space to grow. They can live up to thirty years and grow up to 40 cm. In a bowl, they will slowly die. We must have the ambition to create a large pond where our companies will be able to continue to grow in our own waters and become worldwide players. Digitalis has 4 billion citizens and consumers. Europe already has 500 million. Let's expand that number and give this enormous potential customer base to our country, citizens and companies.

How two Belgians invented the internet... in 1895

About 120 years ago, two men started with a visionary project. The well-respected scientific magazine *Nature* named one of them the "forgotten prophet of the internet"[107], French newspaper *Le Monde* described his work as "paper Google", and Google considered him the spiritual father of the internet. His name? Paul Otlet, born in Brussels 150 years ago.

His big dream was to map all knowledge by collecting every published reference work since the invention of the printing press. This dream took shape after he met Henri La Fontaine, lawyer, politician and pacifist. La Fontaine was also from

One part of the 18 million index cards in the Mundaneum

Brussels and had spent his entire life working for pacifist organizations. He was also the president of the International Peace Bureau, the oldest international organization for peace. In 1913, he even received the Nobel Peace Prize. Furthermore, he played a part in the creation of the League of Nations, the predecessor of the United Nations.

Paul Otlet and Henri La Fontaine were convinced that improving people's knowledge could contribute to worldwide peace. That's why they founded the International Federation for Information and Documentation, which was later named the Mundaneum. The organization created a gigantic archive. Between 1895 and 1934, 18 million files were created with the help of an international network of collaborators. These were archived in special cabinets with over 15,000 drawers. When these archives were transferred to the World Palace (currently Autoworld), which was part of a museum complex in Parc du

Picture of the International Federation for Information and Documentation

Cinquantenaire in Brussels in 1920, they needed more than 100 rooms. Citizens could request information by mail or by phone. Old photographs show how employees in long skirts would search for information in thousands of cabinets. They were in fact the Google or Wikipedia of that time. In order to realize this project, Paul Otlet had come up with a new system for categorizing books. It was based on a code that stood for the exact subject of a book or article. The system was named Universal Decimal Classification (CDU) and is still being used in public libraries and scientific libraries all over the world today.

Paul Otlet, who would have been considered an IT technician today, had other dreams. He was a visionary. In 1906, he wrote a detailed description of portable phones for the brochure *Les aspects du livre* (The aspects of a book): "In the future, the telephone will not have a wire, just like telegraphy. Then— and who could stop us from believing it?—books will undergo a new transformation. Everyone among us will have a small receiver in their pocket. By turning a button, we will be able to align with the frequency of every transmitter."[108] Otlet continued to elaborate on new means and forms of media for distributing this information. In 1934, he published his most famous work, *Traité de documentation* (Textbook about documentation). He mainly wrote about the "telephoto book" which is in fact an early description of what we call a videoconference today. He also described "electric telescopes", connected between us via a network with which information could be sent. He also mentioned how this information could be made visible on what is surprisingly similar to a television screen. Otlet even predicted that people would share files and send each other virtual compliments. The like-button of the past, so to speak. "Otlet was the first person in the world to predict the invention of a worldwide information network. And he did that down to the smallest detail," said American researcher and internet guru Alex Wright.[109] In some way, Otlet was the Leonardo da Vinci of his time. He wrote about digital technology in a very detailed way, although it would have been absolutely impossible to have implemented it in that century.

Otlet was an idealist. He dreamed of a universal city, the Global City. This had to be built around a knowledge center, an artistic center, and an Olympic center, connected by a Nations Avenue.

This city had to be able to accommodate a million people from all over the world, who would communicate with each other and share their knowledge, thus laying the first milestones for global peace. For Otlet, this wasn't a utopian project. He had the ambition to actually realize his dream and even designed the maps of this city, together with famous architect Le Corbusier. Otlet hoped that his metropolis would become the

Two young Belgians, Paul Otlet, the spiritual father of the internet, and Henri La Fontaine, Nobel Peace Prize winner, wanted to collect all the world's knowledge in the Universal Decimal Classification (UDC) system.

location of a global government, which would arise from the League of Nations, founded in 1920. Otlet considered Brussels, Antwerp and Geneva to be potential locations where he could build his global city. For several years, together with La Fontaine, he tried to find financing for his project, which would remain a utopian ideal—even though we have a kind of virtual Global City today: the internet.

Just as they did for their virtual city, Otlet and La Fontaine lost all support for the Mundaneum project. In 1934, the government closed the World Palace. The archives were no longer open to the public, and Otlet continued working on his global archives at home. During the Second World War, the Germans destroyed a large part of the archives. The rest was moved to multiple storage facilities spread across Brussels. Otlet saw his life's work go up in flames. Nevertheless, he continued to work on it until his death in 1944. By then, the world had completely forgotten about him. In 1996, what was left of the archives—which were still six kilometers of documents—was moved to the Belgian city of Mons, where a museum—named the Mundaneum—had been opened. In 2016, it was officially recognized as both a part of European heritage and an important step in the creation of Europe as we know it today. Otlet and La Fontaine's legacy has finally gotten the recognition it deserved and should be used as a source of inspiration. The Mundaneum and the Global City were my main sources of inspiration for the title of this work, Digitalis. I also believe that access to information will lead to worldwide peace and prosperity in the end. Now, we have access to the means to realize the dream of these two visionaries. Today, we must simply have the same ambitions.

A Flemish example of reinvention

The question we can ask ourselves is: has Europe failed to achieve full digitalization to the benefit of China and the United States? I do not think so, and, as an example, I would like to discuss the technological development of Flanders in the 1980s.

In the early 80s, the Flemish economy had reached an impasse. The Flemish government didn't want to idly stand by and, in response to Gaston Geens, they introduced an ambitious plan in order to reinvent the economy. This plan was named DIRV (*Derde Industriële Revolutie in Vlaanderen* or Third Industrial Revolution in Flanders). The measures were not only aimed at supporting the industries that were being threatened by the Japanese robotics sector, but also offered an extensive plan intended to transform Flanders into a high-tech region. In the beginning, the plan was supposed to update the Flemish industrial sector and therefore focused on three new technologies (microelectronics, biotechnology and new materials) in eight sectors (telecommunication, automation, robotics, aerospace, alternative energy, medical devices, agro-industry, and engineering). By encouraging the development of these technologies, Flemish leaders were looking to create more jobs in the industries of the future. Therefore, the plan applied to the entire population. Another example: the biennial technological fair Flanders Technology International was created in 1983 and attracted more than 100,000 visitors until its final edition in 1999. From the third edition in 1987 onwards, the new exposition hall Flanders Expo in Ghent had become the home base of this prestigious Flemish technological event. Entrepreneurs, manufacturers and schools have visited Flanders Technology. It has inspired thousands of students to start studying engineering. This plan allowed the industry to transform itself, and we owe Flanders' current efficacy and prosperity to it. Flanders Technology has become a household name. The posters of the very first editions, with a handshake between a robot and a human being, have now become iconic.

Several companies and initiatives managed to succeed, such as Telenet, Technopolis, and IMEC (an acronym for *Interuniversitair Micro-Electronica Centrum* or Interuniversity Micro Electronics Center). This research institute in the Belgian city of Leuven is the largest independent research center in Europe in the field of microelectronics and nanoelectronics. Today, nearly 3500 researchers are employed there. They attract numerous talented scientists from all over the world and work very closely with the best researchers from the five Flemish universities. Their work generates over 120 patent applications

Flanders Technology has become a household name.

a year. The research center also works with high-tech companies, such as Samsung and Intel. "Our technology is present in practically all electronic chips.

We have recently created a chip capable of self-learning. The function of these chips is inspired by the way our brain works. For example, if you fill the chip with music, it will learn how to compose it. Our ambition is to use this technology in numerous applications, for example for quickly diagnosing cardiac arrhythmia," explains Luc Van den Hove, CEO of IMEC.[110] This illustrates how one inspiring and appealing initiative can lay the foundations for long-term success. Today, once again we are in great need of these kinds of initiatives.

CHAPTER 13

Europe needs new ambitions

We might be doing too well in Europe compared to the rest of the world, and I feel like this overall well-being has caused a certain immobility: we're trying to conserve our achievements, progressively losing our ability to innovate, and our entrepreneurial spirit is starting to drain away. In the modern world—which is evolving rapidly—this attitude is dangerous. We should jump on the digitalization bandwagon now and have to act fast in order to become a leading player in the field. This is the best way for us to maintain our prosperity. But what is Europe's position within the digital world?

Why Silicon Valley isn't in Europe

Europe is not at the center of the current digitalization transformation. American and Chinese companies are in the lead with their enormous internet companies. At the top of the list are Amazon, Google, and Facebook, followed by their Chinese competitors JD.com, Tencent, and Alibaba. The first European company on the list, in 15th place, is Spanish online travel agency ODIGEO. German company Zalando and Swedish firm Spotify are also in the top 20.[III] "People might fear that Europe isn't in the same league as the American and Chinese giants.

And it's worrisome, because Europe can't compete with them. There is no European equivalent to Google, Alibaba or Facebook. This proves that Europe isn't functioning well and that we aren't really a single market. Due to multiple languages and the lack of coordination between national legislation, it's very difficult to build something in a European country and then develop it in the rest of the EU," thinks Peter Hinssen, a technology sector expert.[112] One of the reasons that explains the success of American and Chinese companies in the digital sector is that they have access to a gigantic internal market. China has nearly a billion and a half inhabitants, and the United States has a population of 326 million people. American and Chinese internet companies have an enormous number of potential users, before they've even crossed their own borders. The European Union has 516 million inhabitants. So, the European market has more potential users than the United States, and the average income is higher than in China. Therefore, Europe has the potential to be a flourishing market for digital companies, but unfortunately this isn't the current state of affairs. At the European level, there is no political coherence, and therefore no unified digital market, at the expense of our own companies.

We could coordinate Europe's laws. This would be a good place to start. Someone in Poland may develop great web shops, which are perfectly in line with Polish law regarding VAT, but in order to develop in another country, these same online shops have to comply with entirely different rules. This problem hinders online companies in European countries from going beyond their own borders and developing quickly. This is a problematic situation in a digital economy, where the real challenge often lies in achieving profitability as soon as possible. Cynics say that Europe's current administrative chaos is its best protection against big international players, but in the meantime, we're realizing that it has a negative effect as well. It hasn't stopped Amazon, Apple, Facebook and Google from achieving very strong positions in Europe. These giants have the means to hire an army of lawyers capable of decoding European laws, while our SMEs are slamming into a brick wall.

Moreover, Europe has lacked an important driving force in innovation for a long time, contrary to the United States and China. I would like to discuss the developments in the defense sector. We can come up with numerous ethical and humanitarian arguments against the large investments that have been made in the defense industry, but we can't deny that, in the United States, this sector is an important driving force for innovation.

The technology that was necessary to create the internet was initially meant for military purposes. The same applies to GPS. Even the first moon landing wouldn't have happened without the nuclear arms race between the United States and Russia. Peter Hinssen has said on the subject: "In China, it's also the army that stimulates innovation. Huawei has relations with the Chinese army. Europe doesn't have a military force: we are nothing more than a market."[113] However, it can't be said that Europe doesn't invest in defense at all. "Europe's real problem is its fragmentation. The 28 European states spend a total of 200 billion euros on defense every year. But a large part of this budget is wasted, because we have 28 Ministers of Defense with each their own staff, military schools, supply structures, etc.," explains professor Sven Biscop of the University of Ghent.[114] A unified European army would certainly have added value for the following reasons: on the one hand, we would be less dependent on the United States for our defense and our geopolitical strategy—the necessity of this has become even more urgent in the light of recent developments—and on the other hand, this would allow us to use the money that we invest in the defense industry in a more efficient way. Luckily, we're gradually moving towards a European army. In the autumn of 2017, twenty-three of the Member States signed a historical European defense treaty. Not only will they collaborate more closely on the military front, but they will also coordinate their expenses and operations. This brings us closer to an actual European-wide defense system, even if things could (and should) progress more quickly. Defense includes, among other things, cyber security, the fight against terrorism, and border security. Gigantic budgets have been mobilized. If they were to be invested in innovative defense projects, they could give rise to dynamic changes.

Besides the absence of a single digital market and a common defense policy, cultural factors also hinder innovation in Europe. Over time, we've become used to moderate progress as a rule, but this has put us at a serious disadvantage. Since the Second World War, Europe has succeeded in developing a flourishing economy, which meant a significant increase in general prosperity. The result: Europe is more focused on maintaining the wealth they have built for themselves instead of on innovation. It's anchored in our culture. It's no secret to anyone that the Americans are less afraid of taking risks than the Europeans. This puts us at a disadvantage, because this new industrial revolution will particularly reward risk-takers.

Digital strategy

Public authorities play a crucial role in the digital transformation of our society. They must identify the opportunities, encourage companies to grow, and reduce the disadvantages caused by this transformation to a minimum. The digital revolution is of the same caliber as previous industrial revolutions, in which authorities played a key role due to the creation of a new social framework tailor-made for the industrial society. It was necessary. The huge number of jobs in factories and excessive urbanization caused serious hygiene problems in cities that had become too densely populated, which led to unhealthy living conditions and caused social turmoil. Cities were forced to change radically. The rise of mass production went hand in hand with the exploitation of workers, which forced governments to create more social laws and a social security system. The invention of the combustion engine and the production of cars on an industrial scale fundamentally changed mobility, which required a completely new infrastructure. Even democracy changed: new social developments and two world wars forced the political system to renew itself by, among other things, extending the right to vote. These are merely a few examples of social change that can be caused by an industrial revolution. A hundred years ago, we had to support society in order to help it develop from an agricultural economy towards an industrial economy. Thirty years ago was the time of computerization and automation, and today we're moving from an industrial society towards a digital society. Once again public authorities have an important role to play.

What must happen in order for the digital transformation to be successful? What is the recipe for growth and future prosperity? Everything begins with education. The objective is that every person—young or old—will have the necessary digital skills. Only then can we gain from all the potential benefits the digital economy has to offer us. Then, this new economy won't only be limited to creating a series of startups, but it will have to integrate all companies and sectors. Startups are important, certainly, because they're new in the digital economy. Current startups might be the digital giants of tomorrow. However, they must have the opportunity to grow and have access to sufficient capital investment. It's also possible to simulate the digital revolution by removing legal obstacles that hinder companies and consumers from using alternative digital solutions. We must also have the ambition to be leaders in the field of digital health care. Artificial intelligence, mobile technologies and the Internet of Things open the door for a wide range of new possibilities. It's not only the private sector that will have to become part of the digital world. It's the responsibility of public authorities as well. Both citizens and companies should be able to fulfill their administrative obligations towards public authorities in a user-friendly, digital way. Furthermore, infrastructure must be of excellent quality: every corner of the country needs to have access to mobile internet (and preferable 5G, the fastest connection there is), and the deployment of ultra-fast internet must happen as soon as possible. Security and privacy protection are also crucial: it's not until citizens and companies have sufficient trust in the protection of their online data that the digital economy will be able to achieve its full potential.

At the European level, we must create a genuine, single, digital market, so that our internet companies can grow faster and compete with American and Chinese technology companies. An ambitious defense policy, which will be accompanied by important investments in the European technology sector, can also act as an important driving force for technological innovation.

The law must allow experiments

The digital revolution forces authorities to walk on the razor's edge: laws can hinder the development of new digital technologies and innovative initiatives. Therefore, it's necessary to lay down the rules. In an economy without rules, we would be faced with excesses and this would, sooner or later, lead to serious problems. The financial crisis in 2008 sadly reminds us of such a situation. After American investment bank Lehman Brothers went bankrupt, the entire world was quickly faced with its devastating consequences. "What didn't function well at Lehman was the result of excessive mistakes in the financial sector and in the economy as a whole. After a long period of good economic conditions and low rates—known as the Great Moderation—companies were no longer aware of the risks and a large number among them thought that they could easily profit from the benefits. The financial deregulation made this situation possible," was an analysis offered in the Flemish economic newspaper *De Tijd*.[115] "One explanation for the economic crises lies in the dominance of the Chicago School of Economics, and particularly its belief that fast-paced markets can regulate themselves," was written in *La Libre Belgique* on 30 November 2009. "This belief justified, or rationalized, the deregulation of financial markets in the name of a so-called 'efficient markets' hypothesis. This was a direct cause for the spreading of business models for financial risks, which, by excluding every possible mistake, grossly underestimated the amount of risk within the system."

The same applies to technological innovations: rules and regulations are necessary in order to avoid possible negative consequences. At the same time, these rules must allow us to reap the benefits from technological innovations. It's complex, particularly when the technology is still in its beginning phase. It's very difficult to make legislation about entirely new things because it's impossible to know how they will develop.

Public authorities think that they have to respond to the emergence of new technologies as quickly as possible by creating laws. But these mostly tend to complicate the control over and management of these technologies. For example, California, the home of Silicon Valley, wanted to be the first state to regulate autonomous cars. The starting point was admirable: by authorizing autonomous cars, California would benefit from a competitive advantage compared to the other American states. The first laws were enacted in 2012, but they were very strict. They required someone to be constantly present in the car, so they could take action in the case of an emergency. The result: all autonomous cars that drive around in California are equipped with a driver, a brake, a gas pedal and mirrors. This might have seemed logical in the beginning. But the technology has developed so quickly that all these obligations are now unnecessary and counter-productive. Consequently, Google noticed that it made little sense to have drivers in autonomous cars: they get bored quickly, lose their concentration and are generally unable to react efficiently should it be necessary. The Californian rules quickly became irrelevant. Uber, which is also developing autonomous cars, has moved to Arizona in order to test its driverless cars. In the end, Californian supervisory authorities waited more than four years before they changed their law.[116] They feared, just like the technology industry, that California would lose control over innovation, while the technology sector is its economic driver. But by wanting to regulate new technologies too quickly, California achieved an opposite result.

Digitalization can neither be stimulated nor controlled by new laws. This doesn't mean that new technologies must not be regulated, but that most of the time, the basic principles of existing laws can be applied to the most recent developments, particularly when these are still in an early stage. It will be time to create specific rules when it's clear how these technologies will develop. Introducing rules that are too strict too early often complicates the development of technologies and hinders consumers in using them to their full potential. In many cases, it probably wouldn't be a bad idea to intervene when it appears that some developments are potentially dangerous for consumers. Alexander De Croo, Belgian Deputy Prime Minister, has a good understanding of it: "Public authorities must create a positive environment and give companies sufficient freedom and trust. We don't know what the market will look like over the next 15 years. Even today, public authorities are often still working on the basis of negative prejudices and distrust. They define what is allowed and forbid everything else. It doesn't work like that anymore. Companies and citizens want more freedom. The government should only intervene when things go wrong. [...] If everything is forbidden, there's little chance that people will make mistakes, which means nothing will be done."[117]

Government 4.0

The government should not only encourage innovation and create a framework with which the economy can be reformed, but it should also reinvent itself. The digital evolution offers enormous opportunities for public authorities to increase their efficiency and simplify the maze of administration. The rationalization of the many formalities will surely lead to huge savings for governments. But this requires a completely new way of approaching development. Public authorities are relatively "rigid", which dampens the quick reactions that characterize the digital world. Just like companies, public authorities must dare to experiment, collaborate more with the business world and execute their decisions more quickly. In the past, they could do everything themselves, including developing new programs. That made sense in a time during which things remained unchanged for many years. But today, changes are taking place so fast that public authorities must react more quickly. Startups could become important partners and help public administrations to modernize. On the other hand, governments will offer new opportunities to these young companies, which can, thanks to their early funding, seize opportunities and speed up their development. It's certainly more efficient than subsidies.

At the same time, public administrations must enact good data policies, and not simply content themselves with sitting on an enormous quantity of data. That's why I want to make the case for *open data*. Citizens have to pay for public services. Therefore, it would make sense that the collected data be given back to them. A law recently voted on in Belgium provides for the data collected by the government to be public and accessible in principle, except when it concerns personal data of course. All these data can lay the foundation for the development of very useful applications. Let's take train schedules as an example. If all these data were public, companies could develop apps for travelers. In this way, public authorities could provide society with a great service. Amazing ideas are about to be put into action everywhere. For example, in many cities, people can request the majority of documents in digital form, so that they no longer have to wait at a desk or stand in line for hours. Unfortunately, this is not yet the case everywhere, as some still use their own systems. Estonia is a good example and a source of inspiration. When this small country, with nearly 1.3 million inhabitants, became independent from the Soviet Union in 1991, they resolutely decided to digitalize their public services. The Estonians organize pretty much everything online. It's even possible to vote via the internet. The only things that cannot (yet) be done on the internet are: getting married, getting divorced, and buying or selling a house. In schools, children learn to program from a very young age, which has made this country worthy of being called the Silicon Valley of

Europe. They've proven that it's possible to be small and innovative at the same time.

The European Chief Digital Officer

We have to make fundamental changes in Europe in the digital field. The goal is evident: enabling digitalization. Public authorities play a crucial role in this transformation. I've heard Pierre Rion, a Walloon serial entrepreneur, say many times: "We can compare the role of public authorities to the fire-starters we use to light the barbecue. Authorities must play the part of the igniter. Without fire-starters, it's difficult to light the barbecue, but when the fire has spread, they've disappeared." Public authorities must be inspired by this and support the digital transformation in a highly targeted manner. They should develop a clear vision for the future, create a new social framework, stimulate innovation, and grant targeted subsidies – without these subsidies becoming a permanent means of support.

In order to attract and make sense of all these digital initiatives in Europe, I suggest we appoint a *Chief Digital Officer* (CDO), similar to what Sweden did in early 2018. The United Kingdom has also appointed a CDO, although under a different name. A year earlier, Denmark appointed an ambassador with the task of representing the country in Silicon Valley.[118] A CDO could harmonize the digital strategy and put Europe back on the world map. When the CDO benefits from unconditional political support, he or she could make digitalization a top priority for various governments. This won't be easy. But with clear goals and tight deadlines, it could give digitalization a major boost, particularly compared to the fragmented approach we have today.

But the government can't do it alone. Companies should also acknowledge the potential of new technologies and invest in them. Every individual also has a responsibility to understand what's going on around them and go digital as soon as possible.

If you can dream it, you can do it.

— Walt Disney

It is time for a new ambition for Europe.

Taking action—
A moonshot for Europe

I do not intend to talk about politics, but I believe in a strong Europe. If it's more efficient to settle certain questions at a higher level, I see no reason why we shouldn't. Nor am I so ambitious as to propose a plan that Europe should adopt as is. But allow me all the same, as entrepreneurial icon André Leysen once said with "deliberate levity", to make suggestions capable of inspiring or making both politicians and readers of this book think. If those suggestions could give rise to entirely different ideas, I would also be happy. The key point I want to make is the need to move faster. Digitalization offers enormous opportunities for Europe, our companies, citizens, and our society. I hope to have convinced you of that. Our starting position is solid, and we can digitalize our world with confidence and optimism. We have the necessary capital, and high-levels of education, our know-how is enormous, and our internet infrastructure is generally of good quality. So, nothing keeps us from taking the initiative.

Why shouldn't we develop an ambitious plan, so that Europe can play a central role in Digitalis? In order for that to happen, we have to continue with our work on artificial intelligence. This field is the next major development the digital world will face. "Artificial intelligence is probably the most important thing humanity has every worked on. I think of it as something more profound than electricity or fire," says Google CEO Sundar Pichai.[119] For the internet forerunner, it's essential to invest in artificial intelligence research and in the development of new applications. That should be two of our top priorities. Many other large companies have already started doing this. Why won't the CEOs in our countries and our politicians do the same? Artificial intelligence is an important growing market, and from an economic perspective, it would be very smart to be part of it. Furthermore, we have to prepare our society for the future. Sooner or later, artificial intelligence will be part of our daily lives. This will certainly give rise to ethical and moral questions. The best way to protect our norms and values is by playing a leading role in the development of this technology.

If public authorities were to develop a clear vision in the field of digitalization and the development of artificial intelligence, and the various governments were to align their strategic measures with this goal, it could be an important driving force for our economy and for our society as a whole. Our objective should be to develop our expertise, attract high-level talent, and introduce artificial intelligence in all of our businesses. Europe has many research agencies and specialists, but these are scattered across different countries and universities. We have to combine our strengths and different fields of expertise, by creating a "virtual university for artificial intelligence", for example, to which all centers of knowledge can contribute. The following step would consist of creating a stimulating environment for the development of projects related to artificial intelligence. The final step would involve informing our citizens, and the entire world,—through a comprehensive in-

"The best way to protect our norms and values is by playing a leading role in the development of AI."

ternational communication plan—that we aim to become the worldwide center of knowledge regarding artificial intelligence.

Such a plan might convince young people to start studying technology or science. This will encourage companies to develop faster and to adapt to a new digital world. This will stimulate colleagues to take new training courses. This will encourage businesses to introduce new activities and companies, and this will create opportunities for investors and business angels in new growing markets. This will stimulate public authorities and administrations to offer more efficient and user-friendly services. This will convince talented people and foreign investors to come to Europe.

What we call this project is not that important, so I'll simply call it "Digitalis". But if public authorities were to develop an ambitious vision (a *moonshot*) and our governments align their strategies with this objective, this could motivate a lot of people and create an entirely new dynamic, under the auspices of the CDO mentioned earlier.

Right now, the digitalization of Europe is running a bit behind, but if we focus all our efforts on artificial intelligence, we could get back in the lead. We have all the pieces of the puzzle available to implement this plan. The only thing we're lacking is the desire to do it.

It is particularly important that we dare to dream again. I often hear politicians say the same things: "We don't have the budget," "We're working on it," "That won't work because the competences are scattered" or even "Is it really necessary?". I often refer to an inspiring quote by John F. Kennedy. "We choose to go to the moon in this decade and do the other things, not because they are easy, but because they are hard, because that goal will serve to organize and measure the best of our energies and skills, because that challenge is one that we are willing to accept, one we are unwilling to postpone, and one which we intend to win, . . ." Let's make this digital dream come true. Not because it's easy, but precisely because it's difficult. Because it's the best way to discover how far our knowledge and technologies can take us. Because this will allow us to share a similar goal. Because this will transcend all our differences. Let's dream. We have to go to the moon if we want to be able to touch the stars one day.

Of course, we'll always be faced with practical obstacles when making our dreams come true. What will it take? How can we explain it? What about the right to privacy? And safety? Before we dare to get started, we all want to have answers to these questions. Unfortunately, we no longer have time for that. We're living in a world where we learn through experience, where we fail in order to come back stronger. This is the strategy of successful American and Asian technology companies. If we don't do the same, we're going to be washed away by their new digital technologies. So, we should aim to be part of the conception and development of these technologies. The answer lies in taking charge of our digital future. I am well aware of the budgetary constraints of our various governments, but I'm still convinced that we can achieve a great deal by critically reexamining current investments and by reorienting our strategy towards digital investments, which are the future. For example, we could redirect investments meant for road infrastructure to intelligent mobility, so we can be certain that mobility will develop during the following ten years. Or we can invest our current education budgets in training programs that are useful for the future.

With these clear and ambitious projects, which we'll let everyone know about, we can mobilize 500 million Europeans, so they can face the digital challenge together. Dare to dream, and try to make those dreams come true. That is the key to happiness. That will give you hope and passion. It's the best remedy there is to combat populism, extremism and conservatism.

Have we missed the boat? Not at all. We haven't yet reached the beginning of this (r)evolution. Today, 4 billion people are connected to the internet, and in 2020, there will be nearly 5 billion. In the long term, the entire global population will be interconnected. This means that we are only in the very early stages of the internet, and it's certainly not too late to get on board. Let's get started. With a strong vision and the will to succeed.

Acknowledgements

This book would not have been possible without the support, help and contribution of many people. I would particularly like to thank the following people.

Firstly, my children, Manon, Nelly, Louis and Lola, who represent the future generations and who have had to do without my presence while I was writing this book.

My partner, Annie Deweerdt, for her moral and logistic support.

Michiel Sallaets, with whom I got the crazy idea to write a book one day, and Katya Degrieck, who thought it was a good idea and who put me in contact with publisher Lannoo/Racine.

I would especially like to thank Sven Vonck for being a great writer.

Thank you to publisher Lannoo/Racine, who believed in the book, and particularly to Maarten van Steenbergen and Lieven Sercu. And to Laura Lannoo, who kept track of the process and the final editing stage. This is the first book Laura, Sven and myself have published. A new experience that, I hope, you have appreciated.

To Idris Abercane, Peter Diamandis, Peter Hinssen, Omar Mohout, Johan Norberg and Steven van Belleghem, who have inspired me. André Leysens book *Crisissen zijn uitdagingen* (Crises are challenges), was also a source of inspiration.

To proofreaders and experts, who contributed content or challenged me:

» For the entire project: Mark Janssen and Michiel Sallaets
» Dutch version: Katya Degrieck, Peggy van Laere
» French version: Dr. Pierre Geerts, Alain Gerlache, Lorence Ledrich, Olivier Mouton
» English version: Stephanie Kaup
» Media: Katya Degrieck, Guy Delforge
» Medicine: Dr. Pierre Geerts
» Education: Sven Mastbooms (LAB)
» Mobility: Cathy Macharis (VUB)
» Housing: Laila Landmeters, Thomas Cols (Areal Architecten)
» Retail and marketing: Roel Naessens
» Finance: Anthony Belpaire
» Security and Privacy: François Gilson
» Income inequalities: Koen De Leus (BNP Paribas Fortis)

The copyright revenues of this publication will be entirely donated to the non-profit organization BeCode. This organization offers young people free professional programming training, regardless of their backgrounds or achievements, and thus responds to the critical shortage of qualified IT professionals. We believe that, by increasing their abilities and offering them realistic job perspectives, we can reduce the risk of radicalization in our society. Thank you to Karen Boers for her endless energy, her entrepreneurial spirit and her commitment.

Notes

1 https://www.svd.se/svarast-hittills--kan-du-orden-som-stroks-ar-1900/om/
   de-bortglomda-orden
2 https://www.filosofie.nl/artikelen/ michel-serres-ik-wil-een-leraar-zijn.html
3 Peter Diamandis and Steven Kotler, Abundance: The Future Is Better Than You Think,
   Free Press, 2014, p. 9
4 Max Roser, A history of global living conditions in 5 charts, Our World In Data.
5 Idriss Aberkane, L'économie de la connaissance, Fondation pour l'innovation politique,
   2015, p. 9
6 https://www.nagelmackers.be/src/ Frontend/Files/userfiles/files/
   Nagel mackersmagazine_FR_2016-06.pdf
7 https://www.tijd.be/politiek-economie/ belgie-economie/Hoe-erg-is-het-dat- jobs-bij-
   Carrefour-verdwijnen/9976187
8 Abundance, p. 35
9 Johan Norberg, Progress, Oneworld, 2016, p. 213
10 A history of global living conditions in 5 charts, Our World In Data.
11 Ulrik Haagerup, Constructive News, InnaVatio Publishing, 2014, p. 20
12 https://www.economist.com/news/ finance-and-economics/21707219-charting-
   globalisations-discontents-shooting- elephant
13 https://feb.kuleuven.be/les/ documenten/les17_164
14 https://www.forbes.com/billionaires/ list/#version:static
15 Koen De Leus, L'économie des gagnants, Lannoo, 2017, p. 25
16 Korneel Delbeke 'Zelfs als we alles goed doen, zullen er nog heel veel verliezers zijn',
   De Standaard, 22 July 2017
17 'Fuck work: historicus James Livingston versus de kapitalisten', Humo, 13 June 2017
18 Shaping the future of work in Europe's digital front-runners, McKinsey&Compa- ny,
   October 2017
19 Marc De Vos, 'Futurologie de l'emploi', Le Vif, 29 November 2017
20 http://www.businessinsider.com/ dscout-research-people-touch-cell-pho- nes-2617-
   times-a-day-2016-7?internati- onal=true&r=US&IR=T
21 https://deepmind.com/blog/ deepmind-ai-reduces-google-data-cent- re-cooling-bill-40/
22 https://futurism.com/kurzweil-claims- that-the-singularity-will-happen-by-2045/
23 https://www.weforum.org/events/ world-economic-forum-annual-meet- ing-2018/
   sessions/an-insight-an-idea- with-sundar-pichai
24 Lili Peng and Varun Gulshan, 'Deep Learning for Detection of Diabetic Eye Disease', Google
   Research Blog, 29 November 2016, https://research. googleblog.com/2016/11/
   deep- learn- ing-for-detection-of-diabetic.html
25 https://www.wired.com/2017/06/ googles-ai-eye-doctor-gets-ready-go- work-india/
26 https://www.scientias.nl/hoe-sequen-ce-genoom/

27   Megan Molteni, 'Everyting You Need to Know About Crispr Gene Editing', Wired, 12 May 2017 https://www.wired.com/story/what-is-crispr-gene-editing/
28   'Erfelijk materiaal van mens in kaart gebracht', Gazet van Antwerpen, Tuesday 27 June 2000
29   https://www.genome.gov/27565109/the-cost-of-sequencing-a-human-genome/
30   Roel Verrycken, 'Digitale pil houdt dokter op de hoogte', De Tijd, 15 November 2017
31   Jan De Schamphelaere, 'Levens redden met joystick en pedalen', De Tijd, 14 May 2016
32   Elke Lahousse, 'Living together apart', Knack/Weekend Knack, 11 October 2017, p. 38
33   https://www.vrt.be/vrtnws/nl/2018/01/05/hoe-zullen-we-wonen-in-2018-/
34   https://www.demorgen.be/economie/belg-heeft-een-hekel-aan-verhuizen-b17f6371/
35   https://www.vlaamsbouwmeester.be/sites/default/files/uploads/LIGHT_NL_17052017.pdf
36   https://www.tijd.be/nieuws/archief/Dit-wordt-groter-dan-het-internet/9740753
37   http://www.standaard.be/cnt/dmf20170922_03087623
38   https://en.wikipedia.org/wiki/Berlin_Brandenburg_Airport
39   https://www.youtube.com/watch?v=SObzNdyRTBs
40   http://www.standaard.be/cnt/dmf20170615_02926511
41   https://www.tijd.be/politiek-economie/belgie-vlaanderen/Vlaanderen-slooptjobrecord/9982006
42   https://june.energy/fr
43   https://nuki.io/fr/
44   http://www.standaard.be/cnt/dmf20180109_03289742
45   https://nl.wikipedia.org/wiki/Slimme_stad
46   https://www.tijd.be/ondernemen/milieu-energie/Megabatterij-van-Tesla-meteen-aan-het-werk-gezet/9966839
47   http://inrix.com/scorecard/
48   http://www.who.int/gho/road_safety/mortality/en
49   https://www.bruzz.be/videoreeks/bruzz-24-19112017/video-open-brief-voor-schone-lucht
50   http://www.standaard.be/cnt/dmf20170602_02909133
51   https://www.tijd.be/netto/loopbaan/2018-brengt-mogelijkheden-om-meer-te-verdienen/9967222?highlight=onbelast%20bijverdienen%20inkomsten
52   MIT Technology Review https://www.technologyreview.com/s/607841/a-single-autonomous-car-has-a-huge-impact-on-alleviating-traffic/
53   https://storage.googleapis.com/sdc-prod/v1/safety-report/waymo-safety-report-2017.pdf
54   www.waymo.com
55   https://www.usatoday.com/story/money/cars/2017/11/23/self-driving-cars-programmed-decide-who-dies-crash/891493001/
56   https://www.tijd.be/ondernemen/auto/Tesla-hype-komt-tot-stilstand-in-Belgie/9848116
57   https://www.vrt.be/vrtnws/nl/2017/12/18/minder-verkeersdo-den-door-meer-telewerk/
58   https://www.tijd.be/nieuws/archief/Atlas-Copco-sponsort-spel-dat-ook-meisjes-warm-maakt-voor-technolo-gie/9932722
59   'De toekomst van de universiteit', HENRI, September 2015, p. 13
60   https://www.labonderwijs.be
61   'De toekomst van de universiteit', HENRI, September 2015, p. 11
62   Pieter Haeck, 'Je moet continu bijscholen', De Tijd, 7 September 2016, p. 19
63   https://www.tijd.be/dossier/krant/Te-weinig-bedrijven-beseffen-hoe-snel-de-digitalisering-nadert/9851030
64   http://www.economist.com/node/21531529
65   http://nieuws.coolblue.be/jaarcijfers-coolblue-omzet-groeide-in-2016-met-55-naar-857-miljoen-euro/

66 https://www.trouw.nl/home/ oprichter-van-snel-groeiend-coolblue- barst-van-de-ambitie~a7d57cef/
67 http://www.economist.com/ node/ 13766375
68 https://www.belfius.com/FR/qui-sommes-nous/ambition/index.aspx
69 https://www.tijd.be/nieuws/ archief/M-V-van-de-week-Dominique- Leroy/9914182
70 http://www.standaard.be/cnt/ dmf20160928_02490293
71 https://en.wikipedia.org/wiki/ History_of_Gmail
72 https://www.nrc.nl/ nieuws/2012/01/20/kodak-vond-al- les-uit-leed-aan-koudwater-vrees-en- groef-12154745-a832693
73 https://www.thinkwithgoogle.com/ marketing-resources/data-measure- ment/mobile-page-speed-new-indus- try-benchmarks/?_ga=2.101395017. 95210068 .1518775429-4353 65798.1518775429
74 Stijn Fockedey 'Bringme is een softwareplatoform voor de last inch', Trends, 18 January 2018, p. 70
75 https://www.tijd.be/nieuws/archief/ Alibaba-pompt-miljarden-in-stenen-win-kels/9955161
76 http://www.gondola.be/nl/news/ food-retail/jdcom-opent-honderden-on- bemande-winkels
77 Patrick Claerhout, 'De digitalisering is als de klimaatopwarming', Trends, 30 November 2017, p. 16
78 http://dashboard.febelfin.be/fr
79 Patrick Claerhout, 'Banken doen nieuwe stap in digitalisering', Trends, 29 June 2017, p. 48
80 https://www.ecb.europa.eu/pub/pdf/ scpops/ecb.op201.en.pdf
81 http://deredactie.be/cm/vrtnieuws/ economie/1.2558162
82 https://en.wikipedia.org/wiki/ List_of_cryptocurrencies
83 https://www.tijd.be/ondernemen/financiele-diensten-verzekeringen/Bank-wordt-bewaker-persoonsdata/9757783
84 https://www.tijd.be/nieuws/archief/Blockchain-voor-beginners/9930774
85 Patrick Claerhout, 'De digitalisering is als de klimaatopwarming', Trends, 30 November 2017, p. 15
86 http://www.bvvm.be/?q=fr/system/files/Rapport%20over%20de%20reputatie%20 van%20verzekeraars%20en%20verzekeringen.pdf
87 https://www.elsevierweekblad.nl/kennis/article/2015/07/de-keerzijde-van-internet-jongeren-weten-zelf-niets-meer-1788056W/
88 https://www.tijd.be/tech-media/algemeen/1-Belgsche-krant-op-10-is-digitaal/9793301
89 http://www.persgroep.be/jaarverslag/2016_NL/
90 https://www.imec-int.com/digimeter115
91 https://www.tijd.be/dossier/takethelead/Digitale-revolutie-dreigt-radio-overbodig-te-maken/9881399116
92 https://nl.wikipedia.org/wiki/Facebook
93 https://www.digimedia.be/News/nl/19205/de-belgen-en-het-internet-een-complete-analyse.html
94 http://www.upmc.com/media/NewsReleases/2016/Pages/lin-primack-sm-depression.aspx
95 https://www.tijd.be/opinie/commentaar/disruptie/9972773.html
96 Sven Gatz, Over media heb ik niets te zeggen, Van Halewijck, 2016
97 https://www.forbes.com/sites/michaelkanellos/2016/03/03/152000-smart-devices-every-minute-in-2025-idc-outlines-the-future-of-smart-things/#64da873f4b63
98 https://nl.wikipedia.org/wiki/Privacy

99   https://www.demorgen.be/buitenland/1984-van-george-orwell-opnieuw-in-lijst-van-bestsellers-op-amazon-b0bbea6a/
100 https://www.symantec.com/about/newsroom/press-releases/2018/symantec_0122_01
101 http://datanews.knack.be/ict/nieuws/populairste-wachtwoord-is-ook-dit-jaar-123456/article-normal-944097.html
102 https://www.youtube.com/watch?v=F7pYHN9iC9I
103 https://www.test-aankoop.be/action/pers%20informatie/persberichten/2017/cybersimpel
104 https://www.demorgen.be/binnenland/de-politie-ziet-u-maar-herkent-u-niet-b8c1159a/
105 https://www.volkskrant.nl/media/alle-apparaten-straks-online-zie-dan-maar-eens-een-cyberramp-te-voorkomen~a4530168/
106 https://www.nature.com/articles/509425a?message-global=remove
107 http://archives.mundaneum.org/nl/historiek
108 https://www.demorgen.be/plus/paul-otlet-hoe-een-brusselaar-in-1934-internet-bedacht-b-1412190579150/
109 https://www.nieuwsblad.be/cnt/dmf20180126_03323392
110 https://www.allianz.be/nl/pers/
111 https://en.wikipedia.org/wiki/List_of_largest_Internet_companies
112 Toem Pardoen, 'Wij hebben geen Google, Facebook of Alibaba. Europa wordt het slagveld waar de Amerikaanse en Chinese reuzen elkaar zullen bevechten', Humo, 30 May 2017, p. 54
113 Toem Pardoen, 'Wij hebben geen Google, Facebook of Alibaba. Europa wordt het slagveld waar de Amerikaanse en Chinese reuzen elkaar zullen bevechten', Humo, 30 May 2017, p. 54
114 http://www.knack.be/nieuws/belgie/europa-moet-investeren-in-defensie-niet-om-trump-blij-te-maken-wel-om-eigen-strategie-uit-te-voeren/article-opinion-857021.html
115 https://www.tijd.be/nieuws/archief/Financiele-splinterbom-met-verwoesten-de-effecten/9399416
116 https://www.bloomberg.com/news/articles/2017-03-10/california-says-autonomous-cars-don-t-need-human-drivers
117 http://www.vbo-feb.be/globalassets/actiedomeinen/economie--conjunctuur/digitale-economie/reflect--cyberveilig-heid-ook-uw-verantwoordelijkheid/e-government-de-croo.pdf
118 https://nordic.businessinsider.com/sweden-just-appointed-its-first-chief-digital-officer--/
119 http://money.cnn.com/2018/01/24/technology/sundar-pichai-google-ai-artificial-intelligence/index.html

www.lannoo.com

Register on our website to regularly receive a newsletter with information
about new books and interesting exclusive offers.

Cover: Studio Lannoo (Nele Reyniers)
Cover picture: © Shutterstock
Layout: Studio Lannoo (Nele Reyniers) in collaboration with Keppie & Keppie
Editor: Sven Vonck
Translation: Textcase

© Lannoo Publishers nv, Tielt, 2019 and Thierry Geerts
D/2019/45/179 – ISBN 978 94 014 6022 4 – NUR 740